How to
Write and Sell

Children's
Picture
Books

Jean E. Karl

WRITER'S DIGEST BOOKS

Cincinnati, Ohio

How to Write and Sell Children's Picture Books. Copyright © 1994 by Jean E. Karl. Printed and bound in the United States of America. All rights reserved. No part of this book may be reproduced in any form or by any electronic or mechanical means including information storage and retrieval systems without permission in writing from the publisher, except by a reviewer, who may quote brief passages in a review. Published by Writer's Digest Books, an imprint of F&W Publications, Inc., 1507 Dana Avenue, Cincinnati, Ohio 45207. (800) 289-0963. First edition.

This hardcover edition of *How to Write and Sell Children's Picture Books* features a "self-jacket" that eliminates the need for a separate dust jacket. It provides sturdy protection for your book while it saves paper, trees and energy.

Other fine Writer's Digest Books are available from your local bookstore or direct from the publisher.

00 99 98 97   7 6 5 4

Library of Congress Cataloging-in-Publication Data

Karl, Jean.
   How to write and sell children's picture books / by Jean E. Karl.
     p.   cm.
   Includes index.
   ISBN 0-89879-643-1
   1. Picture books for children—Authorship. 2. Picture books for children—Marketing. I. Title.
PN147.5.K37   1994
808.06'8—dc20   94-631
                                               CIP

Edited by Jack Heffron
Interior design by Paul Neff
Cover design by Paul Neff
Cover illustration by Ursula Roma

ABOUT THE AUTHOR

Jean Karl was born and grew up in Chicago, Illinois, attended Mount Union College in Alliance, Ohio (where during her junior year she produced the monthly college alumni bulletin for $30 per month), and returned to Chicago after graduation to work at Scott-Foresman publishing house. She started in the training department and later worked in the reading department on the Dick and Jane books, as well as readers for older children, and also did some editing of elementary social studies texts. In 1956 she moved to New York to be the editor of children's books for Abingdon Press and in 1961 went to start a children's book department at what was then the newly formed Atheneum Publishers. At Atheneum, two of her books were awarded Caldecott Medals and she also edited a number of Newbery Award winners and books that received other distinguished prizes. Ms. Karl has written one book for adults about children's books, *From Childhood to Childhood, Children's Books and Their Creators*, four science fiction books for middle grade children, one picture book text, *The Search for the Ten-Winged Dragon*, and a short history of the United States for the middle grades, *America Alive, A History*. She is currently semi-retired, but still edits books for Atheneum and writes for both children and adults.

INTRODUCTION
Skills for Success

Why, I could write a book like that!"

How many times have you said that to yourself when you've read a picture book to a child? "So simple. Not many words. A really elementary idea. Maybe it's not something anyone could do, but I could do it. I'm sure of it."

The truth is that maybe you can. If you have the ability to create ideas, to organize your thoughts in a way that other people (especially children) can follow easily, and to put the results down on paper in a simple and interesting fashion, the chances are that you can write a picture book text.

"I can do all that," you say. "But I can't even draw a stick figure, and what's worse, I don't know anyone who can. So how can I write a picture book? A picture book needs pictures."

Good news! You don't need to be able to draw or even know anyone who can draw to sell a picture book text. Publishers know illustrators; it is publishers who put text and illustrations together, not authors. That is, unless the author happens to be a professional illustrator or has a close friend who is going to be the next Caldecott Award winner. Authors do not need to worry about pictures. They need to worry only about text. And this book is designed to help you know how to put that text together.

There is no one key to success in writing a children's picture book text. There is no magic formula for writing the book that will sell to the first editor who sees it. There is no button you can push to tell you the publisher who is just waiting to accept your manuscript. Every author is different; every publisher is different. And for each there is a different road to successful publication. At the same time, some basic skills are necessary to both writing and selling a picture text, and it is these that you will find here.

To succeed as a writer, there is no substitute for sitting down and writing, whether you are just learning to write or have been writing for many years and are simply perfecting your art. Successful authors have often begun writing when they were children and have written for many years before they even considered sending anything to a publisher. By that time they have acquired considerable skill as a writer, established a style, come to know their own interests and even explored the field they were entering. Such a long apprenticeship is not really necessary for those who begin writing as adults, though few people can sit down and write a successful book on their first try. Most people who have some talent and who are willing to work and develop their skills, who have patience enough for self-evaluation and revision, who have courage enough to write and put aside and write again, can succeed in far less time; no one, however, should expect miracles. You wouldn't expect to pick up a violin, never having played one, and appear the next day at Carnegie Hall as a soloist. Writing is not so different. It takes practice and learning. But unlike the violin, it is something you can teach yourself, with a few guides along the way — the sort of guides this book tries to provide.

Writing is not easy. Even knowing what to do and how to do it does not make it simple. But if you have some idea of where you are going and how to get there, you have a better chance of reaching your goal than someone who does not. The ten basic skills presented here, each divided into a series of steps a writer can take, will not put words on paper for you or even decide for you what kind of book to write and how to go about it. But they may give you the background knowledge you need to make better decisions along the way. New writers should probably begin at the beginning, read the book all the way through, then go back and think more about those parts that seem especially appropriate. Be sure to read the chapter on marketing — Skill Eight — for actions you can take that may make your manuscript easier to sell, things you can and maybe should do almost as soon as you decide you want to write for children.

So read what is here, practice, write, evaluate your writing, learn as much as you can. Read picture books, all kinds of picture books. You may be surprised to find few mentioned or listed on these pages, but again and again it will be suggested that you talk with a children's librarian or a good children's bookseller. New books are always arriving (someday yours may be among them), and older titles exist in great profusion; that librarian or bookseller can help you find from among the quantities of books that exist exactly the right books for you. No single list of books would be of value to every reader of this book.

When you are ready to write — write. And when you are ready to try the market — try it. There is an element of luck, always, in getting published, but as has been said many times before, luck favors the prepared and the skilled. It is that preparation and that skill that this book may help you to achieve.

SKILL ONE

Assessing Your Tools as a Writer

Good writers of picture books are professional writers. They have the skills of professional writers and they use them; they also work to increase their skills, to perfect the craft of writing and keep up with the demands of the trade. They are creative artists, who know themselves and know how to use their abilities and ideas and innovative thoughts in ways that will speak to other people, to children first of all, but also to adults.

Much about writing cannot be taught; it comes only through practice. No one can tell another person exactly what must be done to create a successful picture book text. What any author writes, and how he or she writes it, depends upon the writer. It is important, therefore, that first of all a writer look at his or her own ways of working and talents and interests. This chapter will help you to assess yourself.

STEP ONE—DECIDING ON YOUR PHYSICAL WRITING TOOLS

Writing consists of putting words down together in some fashion so they can be read. But in what fashion you choose to do that must be determined by your own inclinations. Some people use long yellow legal pads and write with a pen or pencil. Some people use a typewriter—manual or electric. Other people use a computer or a word processor. What you use does not matter. What does matter is how you use it—how comfortable you feel with the means of writing you have chosen. Experiment with whatever writing tools you have at hand. Which process seems to fit best with your way of thinking and your way of getting your ideas down? Do you need to think slowly and ponder each word? If so, you may want to use pencil and paper. Or do ideas come so fast you can hardly get them down before you forget them? If so, you need a fast computer or word processor. If you are just beginning to write, you may not want to rush out and get new equipment. But if you are serious about your writing, you will acquire the tools that work best for you as soon as possible.

While you are deciding how you should write, decide also where you should write. Most writers find that it is helpful to have one place where they can keep all their writing materials and feel comfortable and at ease while they work. Some authors I know actually write standing up, some write sitting down, and some even write in bed. The main thing is that you have a place where you and your body both know that you are in the business of writing and feel good about being there. If possible this should be a place with a minimum of distractions. Nothing is worse than being interrupted in the middle of constructing the perfect sentence and finding when you come back to it that you have forgotten how it was supposed to go together.

Tell your friends and relatives what time you write each day. Say that you will not answer the phone then. Forget all other distractions. Settle into your comfortable niche — even if it is only the far corner of the basement or attic or even the back seat of your car or an open space in the garage — and write.

STEP TWO — SETTING UP YOUR MENTAL WRITING TOOLS

No matter how comfortable your writing place, how undistracted you may be, how well your typewriter or your word processor or your pen works, you will not be a writer if you never sit down to write.

Writing is hard work. It demands discipline and determination. It demands self-control and self-motivation. Having a great idea can make you feel wonderful. But working out all the details of that idea, writing and rewriting, do not always feel so wonderful. Yet, if you are to be a successful writer, you must persevere, even when you simply can't make that sentence or paragraph work.

Some people find it difficult to assign a specific time to write. But, if you wait for the perfect time, you may never write. So plan to spend a certain amount of time, each day or each week, at your writing, and stick to it. I know successful authors who write at five o'clock in the morning and others who write after everyone else has gone to bed. If you work and take a train or a bus to work, write on the train or the bus—with pen and paper or even a laptop computer.

Set goals. Plan to have a first draft of a given piece done by a given day; keep yourself to the schedule. Then determine when you will have a revision done. If you don't always meet your schedule, you are the only one who will know it. But if you find yourself not meeting your schedule on a regular basis, think about whether you are making a mistake in setting the goals, writing things that do not interest you as much as they should or maybe just not wanting to write as much as you thought you did. If one or both of the first two prove to be your problem, try to find a correction. If the third is the case, no one is forcing you to write. Give it up for the time being, and maybe someday you will come back to it with greater eagerness.

STEP THREE—RECOGNIZING AND USING MODES OF WRITING AS TOOLS

Do not think that just because you have physical tools with which to note down words, and the time and place to do this—as well as the determination to succeed—you have everything you need. You do not. Something more is needed—a mode of work.

What is a mode? Used here, it is the pattern that your time of writing and your way of developing your manuscript assumes. Maybe you have allowed yourself a writing time of three hours a day, but after the first hour nothing happens. During that first hour, words pour out. But then it all seems to dry up. Accept this: plan to write for just an hour or an hour and a half. Or maybe you write very slowly and had planned to write only an hour a day, but at the end of an hour you are barely getting started. Try to find some extra hours for yourself. Or train yourself to think more quickly.

Mode is not only how fast or how slow you write, however, but what results from your efforts. Some people need to race through a first draft, then go back and revise and revise. Other people like to perfect each sentence before they go on to the next. And some deal with their work in modes that lie somewhere in between. No one way of getting words down on paper, of revising and making a manuscript as good as it can possibly be, is better than any other.

What matters is the end product. Find the way that creates the best end product for you. Be aware of your mind and how it operates. Be aware of what is happening when you write, of what mode of writing seems to insure the most continuous progress for you. And go with that way.

STEP FOUR—USING YOUR INTERESTS AND BELIEFS AS TOOLS

Having all of the above tools can make you comfortable as a writer, but none of this will do you any good unless you have something you want to write. The best writers know that the most valuable tool they have is themselves—their own interests and beliefs. It is out of these that your writing ideas must come.

Working with children can help some people develop the ability to write for children. But one does not need to be in touch with children to be a good writer for them. Some writers know children and some do not. But all good writers for children are in touch with the child inside themselves. All of us carry with us the child we once were. And that child is the source of our understanding of childhood and the basis for our viewpoint in writing for children. The best writers for children honor and keep alive the child within, which does not mean being childish, but simply, when necessary, childlike.

Look at the place where you sit, reading this book. What do you see? Probably it is a place that is very familiar to you. How would it have looked to you as a child? Think back to the child that you once were. What excited you? How did you see yourself? How did you see other people? How did you greet the new? Try to recapture not so much specific events and people as your feelings about them; remember how it felt to go to school, how it felt to play with other children, how it felt to go to bed at night and to get up in the morning. Did you have odd ideas about things that you can laugh about now, but that seemed serious then? Can you find in yourself something of that child you were? Can you take that something, that wonder and delight, that sadness and lack of understanding, and see today's world through those eyes? Good writers for children can. They can see the world as a child sees it, sometimes only on demand, sometimes always, because they have never lost some of that childlike outlook. That quality is what you must bring to your viewpoint when writing for young children. Learn to write through a child's eyes while maintaining your adult abilities as a writer and your adult knowledge of the world.

Childlikeness is the basis for writing for young children, but on top of that comes the person you are as an adult. What you once were and what you are now will dictate what you write. The best writers do not go out and search for a topic to write about. Rather, their writing develops out of who they are. And this is how it should be with you. What interests you? Will it interest children, too? Can you tell it in a way that children will understand? Dig into yourself for what you write. Do you love nature and the out-of-doors? Then perhaps that area might give you ideas for a book. Does history appeal to you? What part of history, as you see it, might interest a child? How can it be presented so that small children will understand and come to like history as much as you do? Think of yourself, and think of what you know in terms of what a child might like and find profitable. Use that child within, use the things that have happened to you both as a child and as an adult, and meld them all into a book that will entice and entrance children. Use yourself as the ultimate tool.

However, do not think that this means writing something exactly as it happened to you, even if it happened to you as a child. This may be all right for nonfiction, if you choose to write nonfiction. But if you want to write fiction, putting down your experience with a thin overlay of fiction will not work. Writing out of yourself means allowing all of your life experiences and beliefs to focus in on what you want to write; it means allowing one experience to underlie a story, but not overwhelm it. I have seen hundreds of manuscripts in which an author tells of rescuing a baby bird, managing to keep it alive and finally freeing it to live the life it was born to; these did not make books of fiction. But the core of that experience — saving a life and the joy it gave — could be the underlying emotional base for quite another kind of story: an animal tale, where one kind of baby animal is saved by another kind of animal; a story of a child rescued from some sort of disaster; a story of an older person giving to a child the understanding and help that child needs at a given moment — not rescue from physical disaster, perhaps, so much as rescue from sorrow or misunderstanding. Your life experiences will not generally lead to publishable stories, stories that repeat what happened verbatim, but a real incident may be the emotional foundation on which a story can be built.

This does not mean that the specific material you choose to write cannot begin with actual events. Something that happened, something you heard, something you saw, a catch phrase, a newspaper article, a child's comment can suddenly become more than it was—it can become the basis for a book. But not a book that simply tells what happened. Instead, your mind should use that event as a jumping-off place—a place to begin asking "What if?" and "What next?" The final story should be shaped by everything that you are, by all of your other experiences and knowledge, and also perhaps by the insights you may have gained from looking at children's books, from having a sense of what appeals to children, from knowing what children are reading, what books parents will buy for children, what books libraries are buying, and of how your ideas fit the needs of the day.

Just as self-discipline is needed in writing—doing it on a regular basis—self-discipline is also needed in choosing what to write about. Remember, what you write must say something to someone else and be a work that someone else will enjoy. Knowing the limitations of what can be done may be the final personal tool of the writer for children. You can invent new approaches to old ideas, new ways of telling old stories, new stories that capitalize on the very edges of what is happening in the world. In fact you should do all of these things. Yet you should never get so far ahead of the ultimate consumer that your work baffles rather than intrigues prospective consumers. You could do an alphabet book that did not present the letters alphabetically and you might find a ready audience; but you might have trouble selling a book that invented a whole new alphabet unless there was some useful reason for doing so. You might be excited by the discovery of vast bubbles and strings of galaxies in space, but will a child who does not even understand the solar system care? Knowing the field and accepting its limitations—you really can't write a book about advanced economic theories for small children—but at the same time knowing yourself and using who and what you are is using yourself as a tool. Know yourself. Plan to use all of what you are, within the limitations of the picture book field.

STEP FIVE—CULTIVATING THE ABILITY TO SEE PICTURES

When you write a picture book text, you are obviously writing a book that will have pictures. You do not need to provide the pictures or even find an artist, but you do need to create a text that will accommodate pictures. As you will discover in this book, when you type a final draft of your manuscript and have it ready to send to a publisher, you will not indicate pages as you see them, or even indicate what you think the pictures should be, unless your text is the kind that cannot be understood without pictures. Yet you do need to think *pictures* as you work on your text. A text that offers no possibility for picture variety—a text that is nothing but abstract talk—will not work as a picture book. A mother and child may spend the whole of your book talking with each other—but even if they are always in the same setting and the same relative positions, their conversation must suggest varied pictures that the illustrator can in some way present. If not, your text will not make a picture book.

Learn to think about pictures. Read short stories—adult short stories—and think about pictures. Some stories will not lend themselves to pictures at all. But many of the stories of Poe and O. Henry and such writers of the past do lend themselves to illustration. Try to visualize a series of pictures as you read, each one catching the essence of a given text. Then look at picture books. Go to the library and ask the children's librarian to recommend picture books that he or she believes are particularly well done. Take home a selection of books. Read each book as a whole. Then examine the text on each page and look carefully at the picture on that page. Ask yourself how the text and picture agree. Then ask yourself how the picture extends the text: What did the author not have to say because the picture told what was necessary? Ask yourself how the author set the stage for what appears in the picture but not in the text. In a good picture book, text and pictures blend perfectly; this comes about when the author has given the illustrator freedom, but at the same time set the tone and spirit of what is to be done. If this is a story set in a home, see how the pictures capture that home. Even though the home may not be described, the illustrator will have sensed the kind of home it is from the characters and from the action. If this is a fantasy or folk tale, the same will apply. The illustrator will have taken his or her cue as to how the pictures represent the text from the clues the author has given and from the tone and texture of the text. When you begin to write, remember that not only *what* you say but *how* you say it will help the illustrator create perfect pictures for your text. Rough and abrupt sentences demand rough and abrupt pictures; gentle, evocative sentences demand gentle and evocative pictures.

Construct some exercises for yourself. Think of possible book ideas — not necessarily stories or texts you will ever really want to write — and make an outline of what must be in the text and where pictures might logically fall, remembering that pictures must offer variety and must come at regular intervals. Work at this until the pacing of a picture book text becomes almost automatic. Then you will have given yourself another tool to work with as you write.

Patterns are made to be broken, however. Even if you have come to understand perfectly the pacing a picture book probably should have, remember that each book is an individual experience and must function as such. If the book you believe you must write does not quite fit a typical pattern, then it doesn't. But know what you are doing, be sure that adequate picture possibilities exist, and avoid too much text between any two pictures.

Knowing how to relate pictures with text is a tool that every picture book writer needs to acquire.

STEP SIX — KNOWING THE FIELD

You don't have to know the history of children's books to write successfully for children. You don't have to read children's books to write them yourself. You don't even have to like children to write well for them. But understanding the tradition of children's books, knowing what is happening today in the field, and taking some time to look ahead can make you a more confident writer, one who knows that his or her books belong on the shelves with books that have gone before and maybe with books that will come tomorrow.

Thousands of new books are published each year in the United States, and most other countries are producing them in almost similar numbers. There is no point in trying to keep up with everything that is being done, or that has been done in the past. But it does help to have some knowledge of the field. Many good books (*Bibliophile in the Nursery* by William Targ, *From Rollo to Tom Sawyer* by Alice M. Jordan, *Books, Children and Men* by Paul Hazard, and many others that your local children's librarian can recommend) are available at your library. These will tell you where children's books have been—when they began and how they developed—in the past.

To keep abreast of books coming out each year, you might want to subscribe to *The Horn Book Magazine* or some other respected review media for children's books. I suggest *The Horn Book* because it is designed for a more general audience than many of the others. But there are publications like *Booklist of the American Library Association* and *School Library Journal* that review many books, primarily for schools and libraries, that might be worth your attention. When you see a review that interests you, borrow the book from the library and read it.

You can also keep up with the field by talking with friends who follow it and by talking to librarians and booksellers who see the current crop of books as they become available. The more you know about what is being published and bought, the easier it may be for you to choose what to write.

You want your work to be original and fresh, something that everyone will see belongs to the children of our time. However, sometimes what you write will not be as totally new and different as you hope. Even following what is being published very carefully will not keep you from writing a manuscript that turns out to be very like one that someone else has just published. This happens because authors are people who are aware of what is going on in the world. They are people in the forefront of experience, and they tend to write about what they know and what they see around them—or see coming in the future. You can't avoid duplication sometimes, but knowing what's around will keep you keyed in to what people are reading and where books are going.

At the time I write this, picture books have been "in" for a number of years. Parents, eager to get their children off to a quick start in reading, buy books for them, as do aunts and uncles and grandparents. What they are buying are picture books, because the children they want to appreciate books are children of picture book age.

This trend has been helped by new technological developments that have made possible the production of full-color picture books at prices people are willing to pay. Color television has made full color a necessity in children's books, at least in those for younger children. Changes in the copyright laws some years ago also helped. At one time, a book by an American author or an American illustrator could not be copyrighted in this country if it was printed abroad. That is no longer true, and many picture books are now printed in Hong Kong and Singapore, where printers have all the latest equipment and printing costs are lower than they are here.

There is some feeling that picture books have reached their zenith and that the numbers done each year will not increase in the future. But whether the number grows or not, there will always be a market for new picture books that take advantage of new interests or relate old ideas in new ways. And there will always be a need for picture book authors who can write such books.

To be sure you are one of those authors, you may even want to think into the future. Look at today's schools and what may grow out of them. Look at the social influences on children today, and look at the direction society is taking, the concerns not just of the moment but the ones that are sitting in the wings and just beginning to make themselves felt. It is out of all of these elements that the children's books of tomorrow will be accepted and published.

You have your own interests, concerns, and needs to fulfill when you write. The ideas that come to you are yours. But what you write is likely to be more acceptable if it fills a need at the publisher and in the marketplace. By keeping yourself aware of the world, of changes in social thought (attitudes toward the environment, the homeless, education, the family, for example), your interests and ideas can lie at the growing edge of current thought. And then what you write can lead the parade into the future. Why so much emphasis on tomorrow? Remember that the story you write today, even if it is accepted tomorrow, may be two or three years old by the time it is illustrated and published. Today's ideas may not be right for the market in three years, given the speed with which life around us changes. So know the field for today . . . and tomorrow.

STEP SEVEN — USING PATIENCE AS A TOOL

Patience may be the ultimate tool of a writer. You will need patience from the moment you decide that you want to write. You will need to plan your work patiently, accept patiently the problems that come as you try to get your text molded into a first draft, be patient in regarding what you have done when you finish.

A first draft is not a final draft, no matter how much you would like to think that it is. Use patience. Put that first draft away and come back to it later. You will probably be surprised at how many changes you will want to make, at how many new ideas come to you, at how many words and sentences you want to rewrite. Be patient even when you have revised. Let your manuscript sit. Wait until you are sure it says just what you want it to say in the way you want to say it.

The final need for patience comes after you submit a manuscript to a publisher. If you are an impetuous person, use the energy of your impetuosity in your writing. Make your texts leap with it. But use patience as a tool for accepting yourself and what you have done and in waiting for someone else to accept it as well.

Cultivate these personal tools, make them work for you, and then write the texts you hope will someday become books.

Discovering What Language Can Do for You

W riting is hard work. It means pulling out of yourself worthy and useful thoughts and ideas and couching them in words and sentences and paragraphs that will express them succinctly and that will interest, and maybe even inspire, others. This is especially difficult when the intended audience is small children because the background of experience they bring to books is limited; they have not lived long enough to know the world as you know it. Writing for them is made easier by good writing skills. Just as driving a car is easier for the practiced driver than for the student driver who has to think about all the motions of driving and may have less time to pay attention to the traffic, creating a story or writing a poem or passing along information of one sort or another is easier when the writer has a good command of language. This means that the writer knows the rules of grammar, has learned to put words together in a clear, concise manner, and has developed a workable, personal writing style. This can happen only with study and practice, and just as with driving, practice is as essential as study. Once a writer's language skills have developed to a good working level, the writer does not need to consider all the details of good writing every step of the way; the writer can concentrate on the material at hand and the best way to present it.

You may already know how to write well, but if you don't, some of the steps in this chapter may help you. These steps will help your manuscripts find acceptance at a publisher. *Most manuscript readers pay more attention to a writer's ability to write well than to manuscript content.* Picture book manuscripts, in my experience, seldom make it past a first reader—regardless of content—unless they are exceptionally well written. If you need proof of the fact that writing makes the difference in how well material is received, think of Dr. Seuss. Any one of his books, given the themes he used, could be dull and preachy. It is the style in which the material is handled that makes the books delightful instead.

STEP ONE – EXPLORING WORDS AS PRIMARY WRITING TOOLS

The words you use as you write fall into eight different categories. Some words can be used in more than one way; some are one thing and nothing else. Because a children's picture book contains so few words – in comparison with the number that may appear in a book for older children, let alone in a book for adults – the writer of a picture book must give more careful consideration to the selection of each word used than any other kind of writer – except, perhaps, a poet. In fact, a picture book, no matter whether it is fact or fiction, bears a strong resemblance to poetry because it must say a great deal in a few well-chosen words, put together in ways that make the whole more than the sum of the parts. So here are some ways you may want to think about words and their eight categories.

Nouns are words that identify people, places, creatures and objects and even some abstractions. Nouns generally appear as the subject of a sentence or as the object of the verb. Sometimes a noun is easy to choose – it is a person's name, the name of an object, the simple identification of what is being written about. But other times the writer has options, or needs to find options. If you are writing about milk, using the word "milk" in every sentence would be boring. You need some synonyms – other words that mean nearly the same thing. It is here that you need to be careful. Some perfectly accurate synonyms can seem silly. Try "white liquid" in place of "milk." That might work some place – white liquid flowing through the transparent tubes that come from a milking machine and lead into a refrigerator tank. But most of the time, "white liquid" will sound silly. Try to think of other words that might describe milk, words that will have meaning for young children but that will not seem absurd even to them.

Spend some time thinking about varieties of nouns – both concrete and abstract – and try to think of imaginative words that might be used in place of them, words that children would understand, or could at least grasp from the context of a sentence, words that do not sound silly or stilted or contrived. This is an exercise that you can practice anywhere, anytime: when you wake up in the middle of the night and can't go back to sleep, when you are on a bus or a train, when you are waiting in the dentist's office for root canal work. First you think of a noun, then try to think of other words that could be used in a picture book text that would not only be a good substitute for that word, but might even give whatever it is a somewhat clearer identity. Sometimes the substitute can even be more than one word. "John liked milk. It was his 'drink of choice' with breakfast, lunch and dinner." In that sentence, both *it* (a pronoun) and *drink of choice* stand for *milk*. Have fun thinking of ways to create variety in the nouns you use, without making it all too obvious that that is what you are doing.

Pronouns are words that stand for nouns. They can be used in all the ways that nouns are used. *He*, *she* and *it* are pronouns, as are *we*, *they* and *those*. Pronouns are useful. In the milk sentences above, *it* made a fine substitute for *milk*. But a given pronoun can be overused. Like nouns, individual pronouns need to be rationed. Endless sentences that begin with *she* can get boring, unless the repetition creates a needed emphasis. Pronouns can also be dangerous in some sentences. Technically, a pronoun always refers to the nearest noun (unless it is a possessive) for which it might stand. "Sarah saw her mother and she ran toward her." It is probably Sarah who is doing the running, and she is moving toward her mother. But technically it is the mother who is doing the running. Sometimes sentences of this kind cannot be avoided. But if there is another way of using those pronouns, that way should certainly be considered. "Sarah ran toward the corner when she saw her mother standing there." This sentence is clearer than the first, and would give a child a better mental picture of what is happening.

Adjectives modify nouns and pronouns, and can either be used with the noun or pronoun they modify or as predicate adjectives. Adjectives explain more about who and what the noun or pronoun is. A ball is just a ball until it becomes—one hopes for some good purpose—a *red* ball. If you choose your nouns and your synonyms for your nouns well, you may not need many adjectives. Remember, picture book texts are short: the fewer words the better. When a descriptive word is needed, then, try to find exactly the right one. The right adjective can take the place of a whole paragraph of description. It can create a character or set a scene. Here is another exercise for dentist waiting rooms or boring plane trips: think of people you know and try to find the one right word to capture the essence of that person. Think of places you like — your home, a park, a favorite vacation place — and try to come up with one word that would convey the essence of that place to someone else. You may not always be able to describe a person or set a scene with one word, but when you can, you will have made yourself a better picture book writer.

Verbs are the action words or the words that show relationship in a sentence. They are the words that create movement. And if it is necessary to find exactly the right nouns and adjectives, it is even more necessary to arrive at exactly the right verb. What pictures do the following sentences bring to mind? *Jack walked across the room. Jack sprang across the room. Jack stumbled across the room. Jack fled across the room.* The only difference between those four sentences is the verb. Yet each projects a different circumstance. Good picture book writing demands that you find the perfect verb for every complete sentence you write. Whole paragraphs of action can be eliminated by the right choice of a verb in one sentence. At the same time, it is never wise to strain to use a verb that does what you want but seems out of place. A six-syllable verb in a text largely made up of one-syllable words will simply call attention to itself, which good use of words never does. Your verbs must work for you, but they must also fit naturally into your writing.

Adverbs modify verbs, just as adjectives modify nouns. Adverbs explain where, how, why, and when actions take place. Adverbs can also modify adjectives. What was said about adjectives applies equally to adverbs. If you choose the right verbs, your need for adverbs will shrink. Use them sparingly, and when you do use them, use them well. Think about the sentences in the verb section. The first sentence might have read *Jack walked quickly across the room.* But the second sentence *Jack sprang across the room* not only eliminates the need for the adverb *quickly*, but gives a livelier picture of the action. It actually tells you something about Jack — you know him better when he springs across the room than you do when he walks quickly. Remember this when you are tempted to use an adverb instead of the right verb.

Which does not mean that adverbs are not useful. They are. But they serve best when they are really needed.

Prepositions and conjunctions are connective words. They show relationships between parts of a sentence. Prepositions introduce phrases; conjunctions introduce clauses. Phrases have no verbs, only nouns or pronouns as objects of the preposition, generally. Clauses generally have both a noun and a verb. When you are writing a picture book text, it is important that you choose the right prepositions and the right conjunctions. With the right word, you can convey exactly the relationship you want to describe. *John looked "for" a bluebird* has a different meaning from *John looked "at" a bluebird. Mary went to bed "and" she did not dream* has a different meaning from *Mary went to bed; "however" she did not dream.* In the first case, only the preposition is different. In the second, only the conjunction is different. These are simple and obvious examples. Choices of prepositions and conjunctions can grow much more complicated than this. And the variety of words that can be used in these ways is greater than many writers imagine. To give you a sense of what you can do, find a good grammar book that lists prepositions, conjunctions and conjunctive adverbs.

Exclamations are words that show surprise or amazement or some other strong emotion. Often they are used all by themselves, with an exclamation point following. If there is anything at all that should be used sparingly, it is the exclamation. *"Oh, John, don't do that!"* where "oh" is the exclamation (without the exclamation point this time) is a much weaker sentence than *"John, don't do that!"* where the whole sentence is the exclamation. The first sentence is not an impossible one—it shows weakness on the part of the speaker, and that may be just what the writer wants to do. If so, fine. The second sentence shows a good deal more strength and authority on the part of the speaker. Some exclamations are part of standard English—*Oh, Ouch,* etc.—and some are idiomatic and slang expressions. When used, they should fit the writing in which they appear.

STEP TWO—PUTTING WORDS INTO SENTENCES

Words are the building blocks of sentences. Most sentences, as we have seen, have a subject (a noun or pronoun, usually), a predicate (basically the verb that tells what the subject does or what is being done to it), and sometimes an object (a noun or pronoun or even a predicate adjective or adverb—the result of the action of or on the subject). Within the sentence, subject, predicate and object can be modified by various kinds of adjectives and adverbs. Adjectives and adverbs may be one word or they may be combinations of words, phrases or clauses. *John threw the ball* is a simple sentence. It has a subject, a predicate and an object. In the sentence *John threw the ball over the fence,* the phrase *over the fence* is an adverbial phrase. It tells where John threw the ball. In the sentence *Mary, who was a tennis star, hit the ball hard,* the clause *who was a tennis star* is an independent clause (not totally necessary to the sentence), and is an adjective clause because it tells us something about Mary. It is introduced by the relative pronoun—a form of conjunction—*who,* which is also the subject of the verb *was.* This may sound elementary, but years of reading manuscripts has taught me that, elementary or not, a surprising number of people seem to have no idea of how to construct a sentence. People who cannot write good sentences do not get published.

Writers of children's books are not Proust and should not be. Sentences several pages in length have no place in a picture book. Yet sentence length and style can and should be varied. Even the relatively short sentences needed in most picture books should have many patterns. The usual pattern is for the subject and its modifiers to come first, followed by the verb and its modifiers. But writing can become very dull if sentence after sentence follows this usual pattern. So sometimes the verb and/or its object can come before the subject. (*"Let's go," said Betty.*) Sometimes two equal clauses—sentences in themselves—can be connected by a conjunction to show they are related, and the conjunction used can show just what that relationship is. This creates a complex sentence. (*"Let's go," said Betty, and she ran down the street ahead of Sally.*)

There are many different ways of putting a sentence together. Achieving sentence variety is important in itself, but you may find that it also helps you get across the exact shade of meaning that you want. Look at the three sentences that follow. Each says essentially the same thing, but the connotation of each is different because the emphasis comes in a different place. *The ball that John threw went over the fence. Over the fence went the ball that*

John threw. The fence was what the ball John threw went over. Each sentence could be part of a totally different story. Did John want that ball to go over the fence or did he want it to go somewhere else?

As you strive to write clearly and yet with good sentence variety, you will discover that the patterns of sentences can become a part of an overall rhythm that underlies the work as a whole and gives it the sort of background that mood music gives a motion picture. *The children were merry when they made music* makes a statement, but the rhythm and the feel of the sentence do not complement the meaning as effectively as this sentence, which says much the same thing: *All the children laughed as they sang a lilting song.* The first, with its heavy, stolid approach has nothing to do with merriment or melody, while the second, with its break after *laughed* and its lighter-weight words, its overall lighter rhythm, underlies the meaning with a pattern that emphasizes what is being said. When you begin to understand how sentence variety can emphasize meaning and sentence rhythm can reinforce mood and sense, you have begun to develop a style. A writer who has developed an individual style, a personal approach to the use of language, is becoming a true writer.

Again, not everything that could be said about how to put words together can be said in a book of this length. Explore a good grammar book for more about sentences, sentence patterns, and the ways words fit together to make meaning clear.

STEP THREE – USING FIGURES OF SPEECH – SPECIAL TOOLS TO MAKE YOUR SENTENCES COME ALIVE

Figures of speech are special ways of putting words together that help make meaning clear. Though it is poetry that uses figures of speech most often, all writing includes some, even nonfiction. You will use figures of speech in your writing, whether you know it or not. But it is best to know that you are doing so and to use them well. As with so many other elements of writing, figures of speech must not call attention to themselves. They must function as an integral part of the work, suitable to the rest of the text and blended nicely into the overall level of diction and rhythmic pattern of the writing. Here are the figures of speech you are most likely to use:

Metaphor — an implied likeness — often the statement that one thing is another: "The tree was a fan, blowing in the wind." Metaphors are useful when you need to capture the essence of a person or a thing in a very brief statement. Use metaphor carefully when writing for children—who are apt to be quite literal; but if the perfect metaphor comes to mind, use it and trust your audience to understand.

Simile—an exact comparison using *like* or *as*: "The tree was like a fan, shell shaped and blowing in the wind." You are more likely to use simile for children than metaphor; when you do, look for common comparisons that children will understand, yet comparisons that are not clichés. "John ate like a bird" is an inaccurate simile (birds eat a lot) that has been used too often. "John ate like a snake, one good meal a month" may not sound as pleasant, but it may be more accurate and more unusual.

Analogy—an extended comparison, one that deliberately explores several points of similarity. In a children's book, an analogy might be used to make a child feel at home in nursery school or kindergarten—showing all of the things that make the strange new environment a home away from home: toys; fruit juice; hugs from the teacher; stories; naps—all like home, but a little bit different.

Metonymy and synecdoche—the substitution of a part of something for the whole (synecdoche), or something associated with the matter being discussed for the thing itself (metonymy): *hands* for *workers* or *head* for *the ability to think*. These may be more useful for the older picture book child (the five- and six-year-olds) than the younger, who tend to be quite literal. Nevertheless, there are possibilities: *cookies* for any kind of sweet; *trucks* for many kinds of vehicles; *a night light* for the presence of adults nearby.

Irony—a statement that implies the opposite of what is actually being said. This figure of speech is included here more as a warning than a suggestion that it be used. It generally does not work well with young children. Their experience of the world is not great enough to grasp what is happening. But, there can be times when even the youngest will know enough about something that a bit of irony can be funny to them. *Baby Larry found his cereal bowl very useful* could be funny to a somewhat older child if the text was accompanied by a child in a high-chair with the bowl as a hat and the cereal dripping everywhere.

Alliteration—the use of similar letters or sounds to give a sense of unity to a description or to emphasize a given rhythm or feeling in a group of words. This may be the most useful figure of speech of all for writers of children's books. Good use of alliteration gives rhythm and an appropriate weight to a sentence. *Many marching monsters* sounds ominous indeed—heavy with those *m*s—while *seven slippery sharks*, which ought to sound equally ominous, does not because the words glide along so easily. Well used, alliteration can make your writing come alive.

Exaggeration (hyperbole)—the use of a description or comparison, one word or more, that is stronger than would ordinarily be called for: "His tears watered the entire house." Children enjoy exaggeration and recognize it when it is on their level. Exaggeration is better for children than irony.

Understatement—the opposite of exaggeration, saying less than is really meant. This is harder for children to grasp than exaggeration. But there are times when it can be used—when it can establish an approach to a text that may draw children into a new way of thinking about things. Think about what this sentence might portend: "The moon, John thought, might be too far for a night flight."

Onomatopoeia—the imitation of actual sounds by written and spoken words, and also the use of words that suggest the actions being described. *Ohhh* for the sounds of a ghost; *whisssh* for the sound of the wind. Or an alliteration that captures actions being described: "The sled slid down the slippery slope."

Personification—giving an object, an animal or a quality the attributes of a human being: "The daisy loved the sun." This can be useful, and children will understand—or at least accept on their own terms—a certain amount of personification. But it should not be overused because it may make it difficult for young children to distinguish between what is real and what is fantasy.

Oxymoron—the yoking together of ideas not ordinarily associated. If well chosen and not used too often, these can be fun for children: "Ice cream and trucks took up most of his time."

Puns—yes, puns are figures of speech!—the use of one word in two different senses at the same time, to give a double meaning to what is being said: *"This is no ball to me," said Jack, tossing the ball of yarn he had wound to the ground.* There are certainly better puns than that, and skillful punsters can create puns in their texts that will delight even the youngest of children, providing the words used are words for which children have learned two meanings.

There are other figures of speech, but these are the main ones. They are useful additions to your work, and can sometimes make an idea clear in just a few words, when another kind of explanation might take a whole paragraph. Figures of speech can make your writing interesting, enduring and fun, but they can also overburden your work if you use them too often. They are like spices in food—a little goes a long way. One well-done figure of speech is better than a dozen that are poorly thought out or that do not really work in the context in which they appear.

STEP FOUR—CREATING PARAGRAPHS

Words and sentences, with their patterns of phrases and clauses and figures of speech, are almost always parts of paragraphs. Paragraphs are collections of closely related sentences. They form a unit in the mind of the writer, and explore one part of a total concept. One paragraph ends and a new paragraph begins when a new part of that concept—a new idea—must be introduced.

In well-written material, each sentence builds on the one that went before. In nonfiction writing, especially, the first sentence of a paragraph introduces the subject of the paragraph. The following sentences build on that introduction or further explain it. The last sentence of the paragraph summarizes the whole. As someone once put it, "You tell them what you're going to tell them, then tell them, then tell them what you told them." (What is true of a single paragraph can also be true of a work as a whole.)

The ideas in one paragraph generally lead into the ideas in the next paragraph, which may expand the ideas of the first, build on the ideas of the first, or give collateral information—material that stands side by side with what is given in the first paragraph. A second paragraph leads into a third and so on, until the whole piece is written. When the work is completed, every paragraph must in some way contribute to the whole.

To write paragraphs that really work, it may help you to think of your work in units, in blocks of information, each of which is a needed part of the whole, each of which requires a certain amount of space for itself. Sometimes your blocks will stand side by side, each an equal partner in the establishment of an idea. Sometimes one will rest upon another, the second wholly dependent on the understanding developed in the first. But no matter how they relate, when you are finished, all help to make the final structure, all work together to say what you wanted to say.

As you write, if you include conversation, remember that each speaker has a paragraph (or maybe more than one) for himself. This is true even if the person says only one word:

> "Johnny, it's time to come in," says his mother.
> "NO!"
> "Johnny, now!"
> "No!"

Here each speaker, even stubborn Johnny (a two-year-old?) who says simply "no," gets a whole paragraph.

Characters who think, think by themselves, too. Each has a private paragraph for thinking. Generally in a book for young children, only one character thinks — the others are seen through the eyes of the thinking character; but this is not always true — there are times when more than one character can think — and then, they each think alone.

> "Johnny, it's time to come in."
> She just wanted him to take a bath and go to bed. That's what she wanted. Johnny knew it, and he wasn't going to do it.
> "Johnny, come now."
> She can't make me, Johnny thought.

Or:

> Where is that Johnny? He never knows when to come in. I suppose I'll have to go out and call him.
> Johnny's mother called, but Johnny didn't answer.
> She just wants me to come in and take a bath, Johnny thought.

STEP FIVE – DEVELOPING ORGANIZATION AND STYLE

How do you know where to begin a work and where to end it? How do you know which of those paragraph building blocks belongs on the first page and which on the last? This is a matter of organization. It is a matter of considering where it is easiest for your audience to come into the story you want to tell or into the information you want to give. Begin at the beginning and end at the ending. Or begin with the most elementary part – the state of the world at the start of the story before the problem arises or at the most obvious and simplest piece of knowledge you want to convey – and then move on, step by step, to the more difficult or the more complex parts of your material, and end when you have said all you need to say. Your audience needs to be able to enter your text easily, proceed from one paragraph to the next with a minimum of difficulty, and come out at the end, having moved from one degree of understanding to another.

Exactly what words are used, how they are fitted into sentences and those sentences into paragraphs, how paragraphs work together to make a whole is partly a matter of clear thinking about the text being written, and partly a matter of style.

Style is a combination of the writer's approach to the use of language and to material. It comes of how a writer's mind works. Novice writers – both for children and adults – often try to copy the style – the manner of writing – of an admired author. They choose the short simple sentences of Hemingway, the involved prose of Faulkner, the deceptively simple approach of Marie Hall Ets, or the elegant brashness of Maurice Sendak as a guide to manuscript development. There is nothing wrong with this for a novice writer. Trying to copy someone else can give a writer insight into techniques of handling material that can be useful. But in the end, following another's style too long can be limiting. No two minds work alike. And a writer's best work is done when that writer has a personal style that feels comfortable, but at the same time speaks clearly to an audience and conveys a sense of that person to the reader.

How do you acquire a style? You cannot develop a style deliberately. You cannot say this is the style that I will teach myself to effect. To do so is to risk having your writing sound artificial and contrived. Rather, since style grows out of personality and interests, out of the way you think, you need to practice writing until you write easily and in a manner that seems to reflect you and your interests.

When you practice writing, do not think that you must always write a complete work. Set yourself tasks; try some exercises. Think of a person you want to capture in writing for a child. Make notes to yourself about that person. Jot down all the words and phrases you can think of that apply to that person. Then examine what you have done. Which elements are most important? Which are clearest, which most succinct? How can you put the best together in a way that will capture the person you have in mind, that will reflect how you feel about that person? Try this over and over for different characters. Each time put away what you have written and then come back to it in a week or so. What would you change? Does the writing come alive? Does it recreate for you how you felt about that character? How do your different efforts compare? In what ways are all of your word portraits alike? How are they different? What sounds most like you and still does what you wanted to do?

Now, try describing some favorite scenes and some pieces of action in the same way. Again wait, then judge and compare these with the ones you wrote about people. Observe what you do and how you do it. Does your writing have rhythm? Does it create drama in special ways? When you are not really thinking about *how* you are writing, but concentrating on *what* you are writing, do you balance your sentences in special ways? Do you get variety into the kinds of sentences you use, and yet manage to make them all work together in a pattern that seems natural and easy to follow? Try to improve what you have done and still keep each piece of writing sounding like you, like the person deep inside who needs to come out as you write. As you work, both consciously and unconsciously, you will be developing a special way of your own to say what you want to say.

All writers must learn to make words, sentences and paragraphs work for them in ways that speak clearly to others and yet represent in a special way the personality and interests of the writer. You cannot put one dull sentence after another, write two-dimensional prose or poetry, and expect others to enjoy it, or even to read it. If you are going to take up another's time with your work, you must make the effort to use good words in good patterns, to use rhythm and style, to make your writing come alive. That happens when you put yourself into your writing, when your writing matters to you, and when you have learned to make others see that it matters. You—the person you are—are your own ultimate tool, but language is the tool that will bring what you are to your audience. Learn to use it well.

Choosing the Right Book to Write

A writer may have great inner resources and great writing skills, but if he or she does not write material that is of interest to the market for whom the material is intended, all those resources and skills will go nowhere. It is important for you to choose the right subject matter and to know all of the possibilities from which that choice may be made. A writer of adult books may assume that almost any topic chosen might find an audience. That is not so true for the writer of children's picture books. Yet, even so, the possibilities are greater than many people imagine. For some writers, discovering the range of possible subjects for picture books can be freeing.

Most people think of alphabet books, counting books, and fiction of various sorts when they think of picture books. But the range is far greater than that. The limitations are the limitations of a young child's experience with both words and the world. Yet within those limitations amazing things are possible. To know what books you might write, you need to know what picture books are, what range they cover, and a bit about how to deal with the general limitations of the field. When you do, you will be able to use your talents and your interests to the best possible advantage.

STEP ONE – EXPLORING PICTURE BOOK LIMITS

A picture book text is, of necessity, a short text. Most picture books are 32 pages long, though sometimes a 40- or 48-page book is possible. No matter what sort of book you choose to write, don't be so verbose that there is no room for pictures in those few pages: a picture book text may have as few as one word per page, but it will seldom have more than a hundred words per page — though this may sometimes be extended for ideas that are more complex. This means that the idea for a picture book cannot take in a vast territory. Very few writers, no matter how skilled, can deal successfully with a complete history of the universe in 32 pages, though it is possible to present the solar system, the Milky Way galaxy, and the idea of galaxies beyond our galaxy in a simple text that does not probe too deeply into the nature of each, but simply presents them as existing. Such a book can make looking at the night sky a splendid experience for a young child. The book can be factual, a small science book, or it can be a kind of essay, with the writer's feeling about stars and planets and distances all wrapped up in the whole idea of the universe. Obviously, such a book would not be for a two-year-old, but for a five- or six-year-old. For a two-year-old, the sky, the sun and the stars would be more than enough.

Actually, the thought of a picture book presenting in a straightforward, factual way, or in an essay, or even in poetry, something about the composition of the universe, helps to show what a picture book text must be: simple and self-limited. Picture books are foundations for learning and understanding and do not attempt to present all that is known on the subject. They speak in an entertaining fashion, one that does not preach and does not even strike readers and listeners as being instructive, and they honor a child's intelligence and may open new vistas of understanding for those who encounter them.

That factual book about the universe even for five- and six-year-olds will not talk about atoms, about great winds blowing in the atmospheres of stars, of the differences between pinwheel- and football-shaped galaxies, or about quasars and black holes and pulsars. It will not discuss Cepheid variables or red shifts. It will stick to primary information, but what information the book does give will be accurate and will form a true basis on which to build later understandings. It will do so in an interesting, nonfiction fashion and not in the context of a story (Uncle John takes Betty and Paul on a trip through the universe, demonstrating what is there) because such a text almost always sounds artificial, and the story almost always gets in the way of the information. To help a child understand, it will use things the child can see and feel—the heat of the sun, the monthly changes of the moon, the sparkling path of the Milky Way, the glitter of stars against the dark of night—to make what is said real and understandable.

It cannot be said often enough that a picture book should respect the intelligence of children. A child's experience of the world may be limited, but children of picture book age learn faster and grow more quickly than human beings do at any other time in their lives. Consequently, a picture book must begin where a child is and take that child somewhere that will seem important to that child. Because children do develop so rapidly in the preschool years, a writer can think of books in terms of books for two-year-olds (simple but lively), for three-year-olds (a bit more complex — a bit more exploratory), for four-year-olds (full of answers to endless questions), and for five- and six-year-olds (reaching out to a wider world).

The right picture book can become part of a child's mental furniture, can shape a child's thinking about the world for years to come, can influence a child's use of language for a lifetime, and most of all can help develop powers of thought. That right book is one that knows what the intended reader is likely to know, what he or she is not likely to know, and what he or she might want to know, and that deals with its subject in a way that does not say more than the reader asks to know. You may not have to know all of this as you choose what you will write; you can choose your subject and write it in the way that seems best to you. In fact, you probably should not concern yourself too much with finding the right level for your work before you have done your writing. But once you have something on paper, you need to think about your audience and shape your work as much as you can to the age and interest level it seems to fit.

Within these limitations, and given the impact that a book may have, how then do you decide what to write? Well, you, too, have limitations: limitations of knowledge and interest. You must learn to know your interests and use them. I have seen countless manuscripts by novice writers who have searched the field for the book that "has not been done." They are not successful writers. Successful writers know that almost anything that can be done has been done. What you can bring to a given text is your own enthusiasm for the idea and your own way of presenting that idea. Obviously the idea must be within the grasp and the sphere of interest of at least some children. (No book is for every child — don't ever entertain that notion.) The idea must be one that is in some way child-centered, that can be expressed in a limited amount of space, and lend itself to illustration. If an idea meets these criteria, if it falls within these limitations, it may be worth a try as a subject for a picture book.

STEP TWO – CHOOSING THE FORM YOUR PICTURE BOOK WILL TAKE

There are four, and perhaps five, basic forms that picture books may take: fiction, nonfiction, and two nonfiction varieties that need to be considered by themselves: poetry and essays or concept books. The possible fifth kind of book is the novelty book. Before you begin writing, think about which of these best fits your ideas and your way of writing.

Fiction

When they think of picture books, most people think of stories. And stories are important. They can fall into a number of areas, some of which are obvious and some of which you may not have considered, but which might fit your interests. Retold folktales and fairy tales, modern tales made up by the writer that sound like folktales and fairy tales, take-offs on fairy tales that give old stories a modern twist, stories of children at play and at nursery school, stories of events at home and in the family, holiday stories of various sorts, stories of adventures on vacation, stories about animals — realistic stories or fanciful tales in which the animals really are children in disguise — all are obvious sorts of fiction for the picture book age. But there can also be stories of children who live in other lands and other cultures, stories of children who lived in the past, and stories of children who might live in the future. There can be picture book stories about cars and trucks and airplanes, about older people — grandparent types and people who have interests, abilities and activities that might interest children. Many of these might be fantasy, but some might also be quite realistic.

Fiction for children can range from a simple tale of a small child trying to learn to tie a shoelace and finally succeeding, to stories about family problems, about the joys and sorrows of encountering new experiences; from an animal child learning to accept the need to go to bed at night, to a complicated tale of a prince trying to find the three great treasures of the world. Picture book age children are not all at the same level. As has already been indicated, a child of five will need a different sort of book than a child of two. You need to keep this in mind as you select what you will do and how you will do it. There are no rules, no categories, that define what is right for a child at any given stage of development, but the writer must consider the background that a child is likely to bring to any given material and make the length of the text and the language appropriate for the youngest children who might enjoy what is being written.

Some ideas for fiction will come to you from observing children and what they do — real events that you use as a basis for a story that may in the end not resemble the real event very much. Other fiction ideas will come from thinking back to your own childhood and the things you did or wished you could do, from articles you read in the paper about children that pique your imagination, from books and stories you read, from almost everything that makes up your daily existence. The seeds of stories are everywhere; how those seeds are used is what makes the difference between a successful writer and one who does not succeed.

The main thing to keep in mind as you choose your subject is that the primary goal of any book of fiction is to entertain. But good stories — whether realistic or fantasy, for younger children or older — grow out of universal understandings that are as valid for adults as they are for children. Good stories do not preach, do not deliberately teach, but simply explore an aspect of human experience in a way that a child can understand and make a part of his or her own experience. Picture book stories should mirror life: life in the past, life in the present, life as it might someday be. A picture book story takes the raw material of life — a real experience or an imagined one — and shapes and transforms it into a universal experience, one that children can share and appreciate. At the same time, picture book stories generally end happily, and they give a child a feeling that even small people can succeed in life; the best stories for children are upbeat about life and childhood, even when they portray unfortunate or difficult circumstances.

If you choose to write a story, read the chapter on writing a picture book story and follow its advice as much as you can. But even before you do that, ask yourself the following questions: Does my story idea have a strong plot? Does my story idea have child appeal? Will my story lend itself to interesting pictures? Can

I tell my story in a short enough text that it will fit into a picture book and leave lots of room for pictures? Is this story one that will bear rereading and rereading — because that's what often happens to good stories, they are wanted again and again? Will readers look at the world in a slightly different way because of this story? Can it live in the mind of the child who reads or hears it and help that mind to grow?

If you want help in answering these questions you might want to look at some fine picture books to see how they handle all of these matters. Some writers, when they are preparing to write a book, prefer not to read books by other people for fear such books will subconsciously influence the developing story. But if you read enough other books, the influence of any one is likely to be slight. Read some of the classics: Maurice Sendak's *Where the Wild Things Are*; Tomie de Paola's *Strega Nona*; Tomi Ungerer's *The Three Robbers*; Ludwig Bemelmans's *Madeleine*; any book by Beatrix Potter; any of the Babar books by Jean or Laurent de Brunhoff; the list is endless. Many are now available in paperback, if you want relatively inexpensive copies to keep for your own library. But you will also want to see some of the more recent picture books, to get a view of what is being done now, so find the nearest children's librarian and get his or her suggestions. Plan to spend an afternoon or an evening (if the library has evening hours) or a Saturday morning (if the library is open on Saturdays) looking at picture books and paying special attention to those that the librarian believes are of lasting value. Then think about your prospective story: Does it hold up, or does it pale by comparison? If it pales, you need to think further.

Nonfiction

The most obvious nonfiction books for very young children are those that simply acquaint them with the names of objects they see. These are often the very first books that children have, and sometimes they even have cloth pages so small hands will not tear them easily. From these, young book lovers can move to alphabet books and counting books. Beyond this, there can be simple books about flowers, butterflies, birds, farm animals, pets, stars in the night sky, school and nursery school, visits to the doctor and dentist, visits to the grocery store and the post office, about all of the things that a child may encounter in his or her daily life. There can even be books about things and events a child might not encounter directly, but might wonder about: books that relate to history, to time past; books that relate to other countries; books that explore dinosaurs and other results of scientific exploration; books that speak of what inventions and events may happen in the future. The very young wonder about things, they are more curious than adults, they are full of questions, and simple nonfiction books help to answer those questions. Your ideas for nonfiction books should come from your own interests — whether they are new interests, new knowledge you are trying to gather for yourself, or old interests, knowledge you have acquired over many years.

For those who want to write nonfiction, the important thing to remember is that such books must present true information — information that will remain true no matter how much more a child learns about the subject in later years. Nonfiction books not only answer questions that children may ask, but lay the foundation for asking more questions and learning more and more about a subject. Good choice of subject — one that is important to children (or some children, at any rate) and that is neither so narrow in scope that it does not fit easily into the pattern of a child's experience (a book about how shingles are made for a roof, for example — how a house is built, yes; how the shingles are made and put on, no) or so broad it can't be properly understood by a picture book age child (a book on what the city mayor does may be all right and a book on the United Nations helping children through UNICEF may be all right, but a book on the complexities of local, state and national government or on the total outreach of the UN will be too much).

If you choose to write nonfiction, read the chapter on writing nonfiction, but first ask yourself these questions: Will my subject be of interest to children — not all children maybe, but some children certainly? Can the subject be adequately covered in a text for a book of 32 or 40 pages, with pictures? Does the subject lend itself to pictures that can be interesting in themselves? What will a child understand or see differently after reading about this subject? How much do I know about this subject — can I be sure that what I write will be true and fit in with a child's later encounters with the subject in more detail? What do I bring to the writing of this book that another writer might not bring?

Poetry

A book of poetry for children might contain a single long poem, or it might be a collection of short poems, perhaps all exploring a given theme or perhaps just a variety of musings about life — especially life as a child sees it. Poems, whether short or long, should capture the essence of some aspect of life — love, hope, tomorrow, a field of wild flowers, the peace of the night — or some feeling that a child might have — delight, anguish, surprise, wonder, anticipation. You may get ideas for poetry for children from thinking about children's reactions to both the common and uncommon events of life and to the emotions that even the youngest of us experience. Poetry may be descriptive, but it must certainly evoke emotion and a discovery of inner truth. Poetry is a highly condensed, insightful view of some aspect of living.

Poetry, of course, puts its contents into a form that uses rhythm, line length and sometimes rhyme to help convey its meaning. Those who write poetry need to be skilled in the craft of poetry as well as have the ability to convert a specific idea or event or thing into a metaphor for a more general concept. The form that a poem takes is as important as the words it uses. The two must work together to give the reader — or listener — the meaning that the writer intends. Writing poetry and verse demands a keen knowledge of how to use words in ways that create images and impact, of how to put words together in ways that seem simple but that allow those words to carry more meaning than would at first seem possible. A good poem condenses a big idea into a very few words in a way that is both memorable and exciting.

The keynotes of poetry for children are brevity, rhythm and an illusion of simplicity that masks a great truth of the human experience. Lilian Moore, Beatrice S. de Regniers, Eve Merriam and others do this in their picture books (as well as for older children in other books). If you want to write a poem, ask yourself: Is there any other way that this idea can be expressed? (If there is, then that is the better way.) How does this idea relate to children and their experience of the world? Does it use the familiar to get at ideas that are important for a child's growing understanding of the world and its people? What form should this poem take? What length line, what rhythm, what rhyme, if any? You can get further help with your poems from chapter six on writing poetry and verse.

Concept Books and Essays

Concept books explore some of the same ideas and emotions as poetry, but they are prose. They may explore the emotions children feel when they see a sunset or wander through a woods or feel frightened at a new experience. Concept books can help children accept a new brother or sister, face the dark of their room at night when the lights are turned out, or simply see the beauty of their own backyard in new ways. Some are funny, some are poetic, some are instructive, and some are simply evocative. You may get ideas for concept books from observing the problems that children face, from observing children's reactions to nature or to events in the city, from seeing children's fears and their joys, from wanting to introduce children to ideas that are important to you and that you believe could be important to them, too.

Concept books must be written in simple, but effective prose. They must catch in their few words the whole image of an idea. They feature emotion, sensitivity to an experience — whether real or imagined — understanding of the problems of childhood, and often a sense of awe and wonder at the world and the marvels it contains.

If you think your ideas lend themselves to this kind of treatment, read the chapter on writing essays and concept books, but also ask yourself: Will children understand the idea I am trying to explore? Will the feelings my idea invokes be feelings that children will want to share? Can I get across my idea in a limited amount of text? How limited should my presentation be — and how broad? What approach should I take to make my meaning clear? How will my proposed text lend itself to pictures?

Novelty Books

All of the above forms of books have, at one time or another, been presented in novelty book form: pop-up books, books cut to special shapes, books with holes cut in them, books printed or bound in special ways, books that contain special equipment of some sort — balloons or rubber bands or maps or glasses to be worn, whatever seems needed to finish the book. These pieces are included in special pockets or attached to the book in some way.

Novelty books can be very popular with children, but they are expensive to produce and publishers need to be sure that a large market exists for the book before they will take it on. Even if the market is known to exist, book production and the inclusion of the special article or the working out of the pop-ups or pull tabs may be so difficult the publisher has to give up on the project.

If you want to write a book that demands something special of this sort, seek a publisher that has done a good many similar books. That publisher will have a better idea of how to do what you want to do than a publisher who has never contended with this kind of challenge before.

If you consider writing such a book, the text must follow the general guidelines for whatever kind of book it is: fiction, nonfiction, poetry or essay. And then, over and above the requirements for its form, you must ask yourself: Is this gimmick really necessary? Can you do a book that will accomplish the same ends without the gimmick? What will happen to the book or to the enclosed item when a child gets it? Will it be torn, broken or in some way destroyed almost at once? Do you think it is possible to do what you want to have done—have you ever seen, printed and published, a similar book?

Books of this sort do get published. If your idea is good enough, someone may very well want it. But before you approach a publisher, make sure your text and your descriptions of what you want done are very clear. Follow the guidelines for the kind of book you're writing, follow the steps for manuscript submission, and see what happens.

STEP THREE—THINKING ABOUT PICTURES

You cannot draw. You have never been able to draw. You never will be able to draw. So how can you think about the pictures that must go into your picture book? Well, fortunately, you will not have to draw the pictures that illustrate your text, but you do need to think about pictures as you decide what to write. A picture book without pictures is not a picture book. There are picture books without text, but there are no picture books without pictures.

When you consider what you will write, keep in mind that pictures must illustrate what you do. Generally, your text should read well, just as text. A reader should be able to read what you have written and know what is happening. (The only time this would not be true is when a picture reveals a surprise or a group of surprises. Then you will have to describe as an aside in your manuscript what a picture is to show.) But this does not mean that you should not consider what the pictures might be as you work on your text.

It is important that you consider picture variety as you decide what manuscript you will write. Fiction requires variety in background, in characters and in action. It must be possible for the illustrator to make each picture different and interesting to the child who sees it. It must also be possible for the illustrator to create a series of pictures that will suggest the basic content of the story, so that a child who has encountered a book many times can retell the story from the pictures. In nonfiction, the art must also have variety. If you want to do a whole book on the monarch butterfly, you must give us enough variety — the life cycle of the butterfly, the activities of the butterfly from season to season, etc. — to make the book interesting and useful. Poetry and essays or concept books also need picture variety.

Another factor involving pictures that you must keep in mind as you decide what to write is length. You must be able to write what you need to write in a short enough text to allow room for pictures and to allow relatively even spacing of pictures. And what these pictures should contain should not be too difficult for an artist to delineate. Although publishers and illustrators will not be happy to have detailed descriptions of exactly what you see in each illustration (in my experience, it is almost always the amateur and the poorer writer who feels the need to make explicit explanations of what the pictures should contain — except in cases where the picture is to reveal a surprise, of course), they may very well be pleased to have you send photos or magazine cutouts of the setting for your story, of the costumes your characters might wear, of the botanical details of flowers you describe in your nonfiction flower book, or of anything else that is important to your story but that should be seen in pictures rather than in elaborate descriptions, and for which an illustrator might have difficulty finding correct copy. If, as you think about a topic and do some early research, you cannot find material an artist will find helpful, your topic may not be a good one.

At the same time, your book ideas must be open to interpretation. The best thing that can happen to your text is for an illustrator to like what you have done, to accept whatever information you need to give about things that must be seen in the pictures, and then to go ahead and create something that uses your text and goes beyond it. The best illustrators take a text and do more than create visually the ideas the author has expressed—they add details that neither author nor publisher may have considered. If you were to write a text about Jenny who is looking for an elf in her backyard (and who eventually settles for having seen one when she has seen a praying mantis), you might never have considered how many things in a backyard might look like an elf to an illustrator—even though Jenny does not find them. Jenny may be surrounded by elves and not know it. An element has been added that may make each picture in the book something to be eagerly examined as the text is read. If this should happen to you, you might be angry at first. The illustrator has taken your text and done something with it that made it a different book. But it may be a valuable addition—don't discount it too quickly. However, if you do not want this to happen, you must choose your subject carefully and write your book in such a way that the illustrator will not take liberties with what you have done.

STEP FOUR—KNOWING WHEN TO GIVE UP

No matter how hard you try to come up with the right idea and how hard you work at creating a text with that idea, sometimes what you had hoped would work simply will not come together into a text that seems to work for you. Nothing you do will pull the whole together into the book you had in mind. When this happens, put it away. Do not spend hours and hours working over it. This can be a waste of time. Start something new. It may be that after you have written another text or two, you will suddenly realize why the first text did not work and what you can do about it. Getting away from an idea, from a text that is not working, can be one of the best things you can do to finally bring it to completion. Keep your eyes and ears alert for book ideas. Note them down. Keep a notebook or a card file or simply a box full of these notes. Then when something is not working, fall back on the ideas you have noted down as other possibilities to be written.

Of course, if you find that you cannot be happy with anything you write, and everything is being put away for another day, then you need to take a good look at why you are writing, what you really want to write, and why you can't finish anything. Maybe you are trying to cover too much in your text — or too little. I have known authors who have created long, middle-grade novels out of what they first imagined were picture book ideas. At the same time, all publishers receive, every day, picture book texts so thin and containing so few real ideas that they have no value at all. Think again about what can and cannot be done in a picture book. Maybe yours is an idea that really should be written for older children — a long book — and not a picture book. Maybe you need to write a short story and not a picture book at all. Maybe you need to broaden and deepen your concept. Or maybe you are just too fussy, too demanding of yourself.

When you judge your own work, remember there is no such thing as a perfect book. In fact, a perfect book would be dull. It would have all of the writer's personality ironed out of it in its quest for the ultimate in perfect grammar and perfect structure. So don't put away a manuscript just because it does not quite reach the vision you had of the book when you started it. If it says what you want it to say in a way that makes sense, that will speak to a child and that will lend itself to illustration, then it may be better than you think it is. Put it away, bring it out in a few weeks, and it may sound better than you remembered. If it does, it may be the right idea expressed in the best way possible, and it may be a text that will become a book.

Writing a Story Picture Book

Y ou feel confident that a story is what you really want to write. You have refreshed your grammar, begun to develop a style by writing exercises of various sorts, and now you want to put your new skills to use. But how do you begin?

You begin, of course, with an idea. And from what does that idea emerge? As we discussed in the first chapter, the idea emerges from who and what you are. It comes from how you see the world. And then it comes from events you have seen, information you have read, children you have known, a whole variety of things that filter through your mind. Stories do not just happen, but often ideas do. A story read or remembered and seen in a new light, a chance bit of conversation overheard, an episode between two children on the sidewalk, a child seen at a shopping mall, an event in your own childhood — one of any number of happenings — suddenly seems to suggest a story to you. Your story idea may come from one item of information, one event, or it may be a blend of many happenings. Whatever, one day you had an idea. The idea took root in your mind, and slowly it is becoming a picture book story.

How do you go about getting the words together to tell that story? There are ten steps to acquiring this skill. The first five steps are thinking and planning steps. You may be eager to get words down on paper or into your computer, you may want to see the words unfold, the story emerge, but impatience often breeds a half-told story, one that does not do justice to your idea. So stop and think — make notes, do a bit of writing, but mostly think. This thinking may be done at a desk, or it may be done while you walk the dog, wait in the dentist's office, or wake up in the night unable to go back to sleep. However, or whenever, or wherever you do your thinking, these five steps—in the order given or in whatever order feels comfortable to you—should make the last five steps—the actual writing steps—easier and result in a better manuscript.

STEP ONE—THINK ABOUT PLOT

Every story begins with a plot. A plot is what happens when there is a problem that needs solving. In a picture book, that plot needs to feature a problem that will seem like a real problem to a child—and maybe to an adult as well. Generally, the root of the problem will lie not only in external circumstances but also in the nature of the characters who people the plot. Little Red Riding Hood did not use common sense and suffered as a result. Cinderella's stepsisters and stepmother were selfish and cruel and Cinderella was innately kind—and so she found help in solving her problem. The first two little pigs were heedless and thoughtless and suffered as a result, but the third little pig was smart and he survived. These stories are more than stories of events; they are stories of characters being themselves and suffering or reaping rewards as a result. Who and what the characters are should help establish the problem, and how that problem is solved should depend on the characters as well. In the course of the action, characters may grow and learn, and this may help the problem come to resolution. But the best stories do not aim to teach through that growth and learning—the growth and learning are a part of the story and not the obvious reason for it.

The plot of your story may involve an old folktale or fairy tale; it may tell of the trials of a young modern-day child; it may be serious or it may be funny (humor is always valuable, providing it is humor that is funny to children—that is, not based on a child doing something an adult thinks is funny but a child does not). It may be whatever your mind and your experiences have brought together into an idea for a book. How you handle that plot will depend on how your mind works, how your style has developed, and what it is that you want to tell. Whatever it is you want to do, however, there are certain basic elements of plot that must appear in your finished story.

Plots have a beginning, a middle and an end. They set up a problem and solve it. In a picture book, the problem may be as simple as a small child trying to discover how a balloon gets blown up, or as complicated as a kidnapped princess trying to free herself from the ogre who holds her captive. Your plot must set up the problem in a way that makes clear why the problem exists and why it must be solved; it also helps to set some limits for the attainment of the goal, to achieve some suspense in the tale. The small child wanting to know about blowing up a balloon may need that balloon to decorate his tricycle so he can be part of a parade the other children are having that afternoon. The princess may need to escape before the prince comes to rescue her because she knows the ogre has set a terrible trap for the prince, one that is sure to kill him. A picture book must be told in a relatively few words, so the complications cannot be too great, but they must be there. And they must involve the protagonist in some way that will move the reader into the story and allow him or her to believe in the need to solve the problem.

Many times writers can set up a problem, but they have as hard a time as their characters in deciding what should happen next. As you think about plot, you may want to take pencil and paper in hand and make some notes to yourself. Jot down your basic problem. Then list under it all of the complications that occur to you that might happen in the solving of that problem. Put down everything that comes to mind, even ideas that you feel certain will not work. At the same time, think about how you finally plan to solve the problem. What will your protagonist do that will bring about the desired end? Put the paper away. You may want to try this exercise more than once—even if you think you know exactly what ought to happen in your story. You may discover that you can come up with more than one solution to the problem, in addition to complications that are more numerous than you might have at first imagined. When you have exhausted your thinking about problem, complications and solutions, look over your lists. Which ideas seem to go together? Which complications seem most logical? Which solution seems most reasonable, given your characters and the way they are likely to behave? You may need to think about this for several days, maybe even for several weeks, but a day will come when your plot will fall into a pattern in your mind that you know is right.

When you consider that middle portion of your plot and put down all those ideas—and then try to decide which will or will not work—remember that your protagonist must be at the heart of all of these efforts, and the efforts must be realistic in terms of the story. Furthermore, each complication presented must, in some way, further the plot, even if the results are negative. The small child with the balloon may find that everyone he encounters is too busy to blow up his balloon or even to explain how he can do it himself. The princess may try to find ways out of the dark cave where she is being held, only to come to dreadful dead ends. In each case, though the solution does not appear, avenues of solution have at least been eliminated. Or the middle part of the plot may offer a more positive step-by-step solution. The child may get a suggestion for blowing up the balloon from each person he confronts, each suggestion building on the one before. And the princess may find helpers in that cave, each of whom gives her a suggestion that takes her one step closer to freedom. Whatever the process by which the problem is moved toward solution, suspense must mount. And the reader must care about what is happening. The difficulties you amass for your protagonist and the efforts he or she makes toward a solution depend on where you want to go at the end, who your protagonist is, what relationships with others you want your protagonist to establish, and just what kind of story you want to tell. You are the one writing this book; you are the one who controls it; but you must make sure that you do not seem to be propelling the story to its end. The way you arrive at your solution must seem reasonable and natural in terms of who your characters are and what a reader would believe that they would actually do.

The end of the plot is, of course, the solution. This must come at least in part as the result of the efforts of the protagonist. Adult books and even some books for older children do not need complete solutions, but picture book stories do need a satisfactory ending. The child with the balloon may discover, because of what has happened in the middle, that he can blow up the balloon himself or he can use a bicycle pump to blow it up—and he joyously sets out for the parade. The princess may find a secret way out, or she may confront the ogre with some new knowledge she has discovered that forces the ogre to set her free. In any case, she gets out just as the prince arrives and saves him from certain death. The ending must reflect the beginning, must be a solution to the problem set up at the start of the story. A good ending brings a sense of satisfaction and fulfillment to the reader. The reader must not only believe the ending is possible in terms of the story, but that it is the most likely ending.

Do not be in too big a hurry to settle all the parts of your plot. Work with them. Think about them. Let new thoughts creep in, until you are sure that what you want to do is exactly what ought to be done.

STEP TWO – THINK ABOUT YOUR CHARACTERS

A good story has a plot, but that plot involves characters who live out the events that the plot projects. No matter how good, how well worked out your plot may be, if the characters who make it happen are simply wooden dolls you are moving through their paces, the story will not have the appeal you want it to have. Characters in stories need to seem real, even if they are toys or fanciful animals or elves in a wooded dell.

How do characters become real? They become real when they are real to you. They become real when you know them so well that you know how they talk, how they react to not only the situations in your story but to most events of their daily lives, when you know both their good points and their bad points.

How do you do this? How do you come to know your characters so well? Remember the exercises to extend your use of language: to think of one word that exemplified someone you knew, or to write one paragraph describing a person? These are exercises that will also help you think about your character. Think of words and short paragraphs that contain the essence of each person in your story. But beyond this, visualize each character in his or her daily life, then imagine each character doing things that are not necessary to your plot, but that help you understand the character. Do this for every main character. Carry your characters with you wherever you go. Try to imagine how they would react to things you see and things you do, things you see other people doing. Some writers find it helps to identify their characters with people they know, or to combine certain aspects of several people in one character (even fanciful animals can take on characteristics in this way, since many times they are really people in disguise). Other writers prefer to create characters with no reference at all to friends, acquaintances or relatives. But however you create your characters, remember that whatever they do in your story, whatever they say, must fit with the person you have come to know. You cannot make your characters do things that they would not typically do, just to satisfy your plot. If your characters and your plot cannot work together, one or the other is wrong.

Do not think, however, that when you come to writing your story you will include all that you know about your characters. In fact, you may not even use those one-word descriptions. But by having come to know your characters so well, you will be able in the telling of your story to make them act in accord with a nature that is all their own. Character does not come across in a story through what the writer tells us about a person, but through the way that character acts and speaks. A small child will speak in a different fashion from an older child. If the child with the balloon is shy, he may gently pull at his mother's dress when he wants her attention; if he is brash, he will stride up to her and demand an answer. If the princess is sweet and gentle, she may move more cautiously in that cave, and her approach to the various characters she meets will be quite different from a take-charge sort of princess, who will be independent and brisk and maybe even demanding. Every word you use to describe the actions and the speech of each character must reflect the nature of that character. It is in this way, and not by description, that you will convince your reader that your characters are the people you want them to be.

When you consider your plot and then think about its characters, remember that the two are mutually dependent; they must be totally in tune with each other. What happens in the plot must happen because of the people who are living through the events you picture. Who your people are must determine how the plot proceeds, and how plot proceeds must determine the kind of people about whom you are writing. So as the characters become real to you, you must test them against your plot and let both plot and characters shape your thinking about the story you are going to tell. Whether your characters are based on real people or simply on strong mental images of the actors in your plot, they must be consistent; they must live the plot as they would live it in those wider lives you have imagined. They may grow in knowledge and experience and even in character traits as they live out your plot, but they don't surprise you or your readers with traits that come out of nowhere to create the final solution of your plot. They are always true to themselves.

As you think about your characters, write down words that describe them, make lists of words that describe how they move, words that might be a part of their speech, words that might exemplify the way they think. As you make your lists, remember that your words must tell your story — every single word must carry the story one step further — that the words of speech and action must define your characters, but you cannot use words that do not fit the general tone of your work just because they do what you need at that point. The right word is always the one that blends with the others, not the one that calls attention to itself, no matter how well it may carry the meaning you need to convey.

One of the reasons that writing a picture book text is so difficult is that there is no room for long descriptions. But be assured that if you have come to understand your characters well, and if the plot is the perfect vehicle for them, you will not need to describe them. The simple telling of your story will tell all that the reader needs to know about who and what they are.

STEP THREE — THINK ABOUT BACKGROUND

No matter what kind of story you are writing, it must take place somewhere. Nothing happens in a vacuum — unless your characters are dust grains reacting to the problems housecleaning creates for them in a vacuum cleaner.

Just as you reflected on plot and came to know your characters, you must consider the story background. Is yours a story about a child at home? Then what is that home like? How many other children are in the family? You should know this even if some will not appear in your story at all. Is Mother home during the day or does she work? If she works, who takes care of the children? Is this the home of a poor, middle-class, or rich family? What are the goals and ideals of that family? All these things will influence your plot and the nature of your characters.

It is best to put your characters into a situation that feels comfortable to you — some place you know and understand, a place where even the dark corners are familiar. If your story must be set in a far or imaginary place, you must come to know that place as well as you know your characters and your plot. If it is a real place, find out all you can about it — read books about it, visit it if you can, see films that explore it, if such films are available. If it is an imaginary place, draw maps of the area, even of parts that may not appear in your story. Know where people live, how they get their food (do those dragons feed on the local population or a distant one?), how their structures appear (do those toadstools used as houses have sides?), what forms of transportation they use (are those spaceships large or small?), and how the general landscape appears (why do the rivers run uphill?).

Finally, home in on the exact places where your action will take place. What details of the background will be important to your story? How can you make those details apparent to your readers without having to indulge in lengthy descriptions? Remember, in a picture book, there is little room in the text for description. And, of course, remember that the artist will be helpful to you in creating background. But if the artist is to picture the scenes of your story in the ways that they appear to you, the text must give the artist clues that he or she can follow. Surprisingly, setting can display itself just as character does, through plot and action.

> Tommy raced through the apartment looking for his mother. Living room? Not there! Bedroom? Not there! Kitchen? Not there! And she certainly wasn't in his bedroom. Where was she? There was no place else to look!

Here you see where Tommy lives as you also encounter his problem — where is his mother? Once again, you may want to make some lists for yourself. Begin by thinking about your plot. Where does each phase of the plot take place? What actions are dependent on the physical feature of that place and on the other aspects of your background? How can you express those actions in ways that will show setting? Make notes to yourself, write down words that may help, but just as with showing character, remember that the words you use must blend with the whole.

There are times, of course, when a certain amount of description is necessary, especially when background varies from the expected norm. If the land in which your story takes place substitutes purple for green, the reader will need to be told this — and the illustrator will be grateful for your having put it into the text so no one will think it is his or her idea. But if you do have such an aberration as a part of your story, there must be good reason for it. Backgrounds should not deviate unduly from what is expected unless the change serves a real purpose. Purple trees cannot exist just to be purple trees: they must be important to the story — the end of a magical search, or the subject of controversy. And because they are a part of the plot, they really will not need as much explanation as you might think.

> Purple! The trees were purple! Dina could not understand it. She was sure those trees had been green yesterday. Why were they purple today? What was happening? Did it have anything to do with that strange little man she had seen walking down the lane yesterday, pointing at each tree? But why would he want to turn trees purple?

Here, without having to describe very much, we have purple trees that define a mystery, raise questions and begin a plot.

Like characters, you can create backgrounds from real places you know, from places you would like to know, or from places that exist only to serve the characters and the plot. But in any case a background must fit the story, and be a likely setting for the characters who live there. Whether the setting is cozy, dangerous, far-flung, or small and intimate, the reader must believe that what happens in your plot could happen there, and that the characters who live in your plot also live in your setting. Do not strive for exotic settings when one closer to home will work just as well. At the same time, exotic adventures are generally more believable in a place that is a little distant from the usual.

STEP FOUR—THINK ABOUT PATTERN

What should the basic structure of your story be? Consider first the various ways in which your story might be told: first person (to bring the reader into the center of the action) or third person (a story that takes readers out of themselves); past tense (the usual form) or present tense (to give the story immediacy); in a typical folktale style (*Once upon a time*, etc.), in a breezy modern style (*"Cool, man, cool. Chill out."*) or in something in between; with a minimum of words (basic action in rhythmic prose) or with a maximum of words (flowing sentences and carefully delineated scenes)? The pattern and rhythm of your telling — the mode you choose for the writing of your text — must be a part of what you have decided about plot, character and background. What style best fits the story you want to tell? Try several samples if you like. See which means of telling lets you incorporate character and setting into your plot in the easiest fashion. Which style of telling most characterizes the story itself? A dreamy, imaginative tale surely should not be told in short, brisk sentences, but it might be told in first person if one person is doing the dreaming and imagining. A story of a fight between two three-year-olds will not use long, evocative sentences — it may use short choppy phrases to indicate the anger and the action. Think about what form, what pattern, would best suit your story.

Next, think about where your story really begins. In my experience, writers, especially new writers, think they have to do a lot of explaining before they really get into the meat of the story. Nothing could be further from the truth. Readers want to know right away what is going to happen in your story. Action and plot should begin on the very first page, in the very first paragraph. Think about your story. Where does the action begin, not just any action, but the real core of your action? That is where your text must begin, too. And anything that the reader needs to know about your characters and your setting must come through in the way you delineate that action.

> Bobby sat on his tricycle in front of his house and looked at the balloon in his hand. He had seen the bigger kids blow up a balloon. It looked easy. But no matter how hard he blew, nothing happened. Would they let him in the block parade if he didn't even have a balloon to carry?

From this you know that Bobby is young, he rides a tricycle, he lives in a house, and probably he lives in a suburban area. You also know what his problem is and you know that there are bigger children around.

Then think about how many action sequences, how many separate scenes, you need to tell your story. Is the story continuous or are there breaks between episodes? Is there more than one main character? Do they work together or do they work separately — how much of the story does each require? Do we see both the princess in her cave and the prince coming nearer and nearer, shifting scenes from one to the other? How often does this happen? You will not want to shift scenes too often or in too confusing a way for young readers to grasp. But if it is really necessary, you can delineate two sets of episodes, like cars on two roads that will meet at a crossroads. But think, would it be better if the reader didn't know where the prince was — if tension builds because he might be caught in that ogre's trap at any moment.

Think about the pattern of action that will tell your story in the simplest way possible, at the same time creating the greatest amount of interest and tension in the reader before the problem is finally solved. Keep the pattern spare, but at the same time tell the reader as much as is necessary to understand the story. It is important that each episode of the story build on the one that went before and carry the reader along to the next episode. Pretend you are climbing a hill: each event in the story takes you up one switchback until, when the moment of plot resolution comes, you are at the top of the hill. The way back down the hill is by fast train — once the top is reached there should be little more to say.

So think about your story. Make notes about it. Make an outline, maybe several outlines trying out different ways you could plan for the action to happen. Figure out the minimum number of steps you need to get from beginning to end, keeping in mind that you don't want to strip the story of exciting action, but remembering that each action sequence must further the plot, remembering that simplicity is better than undue complication, providing there is adequate tension.

If you are writing the boy and the balloon story you might try several approaches. If yours is a brash child you might set up the following outline for a 28-page story:

1. Acquiring a balloon — given or just taking — demanding? — 3 pages
2. The attempt to blow it up — 2 pages
3. Approaches to others for help — 12 pages — refusals for what reasons?
4. Further attempts — using some helpful suggestions — 4 pages
5. Success — 4 pages
6. Parade — victory — 3 pages

If your child were not so brash, but still persistent, you might alter the above to get one good suggestion from each person he or she approaches — and when all are put together the good result is obtained—or one person might send the child to the next person, and the final person would have the answer.

If you were writing an outline for the princess story, the same would apply—how your story moved would depend upon the nature of the princess herself. If you have a very brisk and independent princess your outline for a 28-page story might look like this:

1. Set up situation—either being with princess in cave or seeing her captured and put in cave—mad and struggling—3 pages

2. Princess determined to find her way out, sets forth—using magic light to guide her way or feeling her way? —2 pages

3. Princess encounters numerous cave denizens, from insects to ogres and dragons or whatever—demands help from each— gets a word of advice from each, some helpful, some not—12 pages

4. Princess decides she has to do this on her own—she uses information she has been given, sets out in a determined fashion and finds several dead ends—4 pages

5. Princess finds the ogre himself, and with knowledge she has gained confronts him and defeats him—4 pages

6. Princess sets out to save prince—since the destructive cycle is set—she does and they either go off into the sunset, or she sends him off because he is so weak she had to save him and she wants a stronger prince—3 pages

If your princess were a more demure person, she might inquire nicely for help from each character she meets in the cave, and they might all be so impressed by her that they would come with her to confront the ogre and save the prince. This princess will surely go off with the prince at the end, and maybe all of her new friends will go with her, too.

As you contemplate your story and your characters, figure out the quickest and most reasonable way to get from one action sequence to the next without making the story seem jumpy and certainly without leaving out information that the reader needs to know. Setting the scene well in the first couple of pages, indicating the nature of your main character and the way in which he or she intends to solve the problem can help a great deal in making the sequence of events move easily without your needing to include unduly long explanations.

You should also note that it is important for you to consider what your ending will be and to work up to it in a logical fashion. Is the ending a surprise? Does the princess reject the prince because he is so weak, after she has saved him? If so, the character of the princess all along must make this ending reasonable. You must build the likelihood of that ending into what you do, even though the ending is a surprise. At each encounter with another being, the princess must show that she is strong and in control and has no time for weaklings. If we come to the final conclusion gradually, we are prepared for what will happen, but the reader awaits the final release of confirmation from you, the storyteller, to relate what really did happen. How you approach the ending and resolve the plot must belong to the story as a whole. And that resolution must seem reasonable and logical in terms of the whole—it cannot seem tacked on or be arrived at simply because that's the way you want the story to end. Remember, it is your characters and not you who are living this story, and what they do and how they do it must determine what happens in the end. If you were writing the boy and the balloon story, the brash child would never give up, but the shy child might until rescued by someone who cares about him.

Pattern is the glue that weaves plot, characters and background into that cohesive whole your story must present. Pattern involves not only plot, characters and background, however, but also tone and pace, rhythm and ambience. All of this together tells the reader how to react to what is happening in the story. Your voice must reach the reader through your written words, sentences and paragraphs—the tools of your trade that you practiced and perfected earlier. If you have learned to use them well, the patterns you construct, or better still the patterns you allow your characters to build, will make for stories that come alive in the minds of children and live there for years to come.

STEP FIVE—THINK ABOUT WHAT YOU HAVE DONE SO FAR

Now is the moment to consider what you are really writing. Are you writing a picture book text, or is it going to take more text than the normal picture book allows to tell the story you have worked out? Does the action you have plotted lend itself to pictures and to picture variety? If all the scenes take place in exactly the same location, or if the story revolves around the protagonist having a series of abstract ideas seated on a chair in a bedroom, even the greatest artist in the world may not be able to create enough picture variety to keep a child interested. Pictures must change from page to page to keep readers — and more important, listeners — interested. Listeners examine pictures while text is being read; they need variety.

Go beyond pictures. Does the story have enough amusement, depth, action or psychological stimulation to bring a child back to it again and again, finding each time the same satisfaction he or she found the first time — or better yet, finding more and more things about the story to enjoy? Will the story stir an emotion — joy, sadness, anger, fear, whatever may be appropriate? A good text always arouses some emotion in the mind of the person for whom it is intended. I have known authors who wept as they wrote when something sad was happening in the story. Probably their readers wept, too. Your story will carry emotion if you feel an emotion yourself.

After all this thought, do you still feel good about the story? Does it still hold appeal for you? Do you look forward to writing it? Do you see the story in your mind as a whole and does it seem to have an existence of its own? Is this a story you would like to tell — or to hear — again and again? Are you, yourself, involved in this story — does it come from deep within you — do you feel a kinship with it? Are you revealing something of the core of yourself in this story? Think about it. Wonder about it. And if you feel a strong *yes* inside, then you are ready to write.

The next five steps are writing and rewriting steps. If the thinking steps have done their job, the writing steps should be quite easy. One word of caution: Pace the thinking stages well; do not skip over them too casually; at the same time, do not think so long that the story never gets written. Understand your own thought processes and work with them, beginning to write at the moment the story seems fleshed out and full to you — when you see it as a whole and know it well enough that you are almost positive of exactly how it should be done, but before you have examined and reexamined it to the point that it no longer excites you.

STEP SIX—WRITING A FIRST DRAFT

By now your story should be like a ripe apple, ready to fall, or like an egg ready to crack open and reveal the chick inside. You should know how your plot unfolds—how the problem is established, what complications ensue, and how the whole is resolved. You should know how your characters feel about what is happening to them, how they react to each turn of the plot; you must believe they are really involved in what is happening and that their actions as the plot evolves are the logical ones for the people they are. You know all of the elements of background, why the story is set there and how it figures into the plot and into the behavior of the characters. You see the pattern that fits the telling of the story: know where it should begin, the pace at which it should proceed, and the way the resolution of the plot must be handled.

Besides the ideas in your mind, you probably have lists of action words and words to be used in speech, all of which will delineate your characters without your having to spend precious words and sentences describing them. You may have various approaches to parts of the story written out: sentences and even paragraphs that have helped you decide how the story should be put together and written down. You may have an outline. You may have notes on elements of background that need to enter the story through action and speech and thought. All of these things have helped you get to the point where you now are. *Put them all away.* Don't use them as a primary tool when you write. Refer to them only when you need a specific word and can't think of it. You will come back to all of this again when your first draft is finished. But you will not plunk any of this bodily into what you do now. Why not? Because what you have amassed are bits and pieces that may or may not work together as you write. What you need to do is to sit down and, using all the information you have about your story, simply tell it as you know it in a way that is smooth and consistent.

Now is the time for the story to tell itself. And it will, if you have done your thinking well. Your mind will have taken all of that information and made it into something even more special than you could have imagined. Don't worry if, as you write, not all of the things you thought about get into the story. Maybe some of them don't really belong. Let the story free itself and get down onto paper or into your computer or whatever.

Of course, this doesn't happen by magic. And it may not be easy. The words and the sentences and the paragraphs may not spill out without your thinking and working and searching for the right word, the right sentence pattern, the right rhythm, the right way to say something so that character and background as well as action are revealed. But don't force the story to come. If you must struggle too hard to get your story down, you may need more thinking time. Or you may simply need to put out of your mind all you have learned. Now is not the time to try to remember all the elements of good writing. Let what you have learned show itself naturally in what you write, but don't let it inhibit you. If you try to remember all the rules and all the tricks of writing that you have ever learned and follow them, your writing will sound stilted and false. Learn the rules, learn the tricks, learn all about your story, and then sit down and write unself-consciously — letting happen what will. (After all, no one but you will see what you are doing; before anyone else reads it, you can and will revise.)

As we discussed in the first chapter — Skill One — you may choose to write with pencil or pen on paper, to type the story on a manual or electric typewriter, or to feed your sentences, paragraphs and pages into the computer. You may perfect each sentence before going to the next, or rip through the whole story in one quick sitting, knowing that endless revisions lie ahead. It doesn't matter how you choose to write. What does matter now is that you sit down and do it.

Do you begin at the beginning to tell the story? Most people do, especially with picture book stories. But not everyone does, and you don't have to if another approach feels more comfortable to you. Some people write the ending first, so they know exactly where they are going. Other people write various sequences, out of order, and later pull them together in the way they should go, writing whatever transitions are needed. Do what comes naturally, letting the story reveal itself to you now as if it is brand new. Enjoy telling it to yourself, as you hope others will enjoy reading it.

Try to put down only what needs to be in writing to capture the essence of your tale. You know the story in great depth, but you don't have to tell your readers everything you know. What they need is the heart of the story, the core, the kernel, the visible action from the time it begins until the plot resolves itself. This you will present in words that give life to the characters and the action: you know what those words are — you have lists of them, but if your thinking was true, those lists are in your mind and the ones you really need most will appear when and where they belong. If you know your characters, their speech and the words that describe how they move and how they think will all reveal to your readers who they are and why they are a part of your story. Concentrate on your people and on what happens to them; see the action of your plot in your mind as you write; describe the sequences of your plot in words that carry the emotions your characters feel. A poorly thrown ball, for example, does not just "break a window," it "crunches into a window" or "Jim shuddered with the glass as it broke."

No matter how splendid your story may be, if the words you use and the sentences you construct do not convey this splendor, readers are not likely to respond as you expect. Words and phrases that suit the material—in sounds as well as meaning—are what make your story come alive; soft, gentle words and phrases in rolling measures for soft and gentle events; brisk, snappy words in short, stubby phrases for quick action; always make your way of telling fit the events you are recounting. Do think about language as you write, even as you are letting your story reveal itself.

Keep in mind all of the things you know should be a part of your story; but don't think too much. Write. Basic thinking time is past; this is the time to put all of those thoughts to work. You may want to use some of those lists of words you made. You will surely want to keep in mind the outline you made, if you made one, and you may even find yourself able to use some of the phrases you developed. But most of all, you will want to ease your story along in the way it must go, without too much outside interference.

In the overall picture, let the story tell itself. Put down the words that come to you, as they come to you. If you are telling the story of the small boy and the balloon, think about the core of the story—the boy wanting to blow up that balloon, his many attempts, his final success. This is your story. Hold that total frame in your head, then write the words that best fill that frame with a picture, keeping the picture as uncluttered as possible. Keep the central image clear and sharp. This is a single picture, not a diptych or a triptych: you don't need to tell us what your small boy ate for breakfast, what his sister did last night or where his mother works—unless some of these contribute heavily to the main picture. But you do need to tell us what the boy wants to do, why this is important to him, how he goes about doing it, what happens each time he fails, and how he finally succeeds and the joyous event that follows (the parade, of which he is a part). Keeping the story as you have developed it in mind, write the words needed to tell it, the words that tell it in the shortest way possible. Again, try to picture the events of the story in your mind and then describe those events in your writing.

If you think of your book as being for a very young child, you will probably write fewer words and leave more of the action to the work of the illustrator. In writing that balloon book you might begin:

> Mary had a big balloon on the back of her trike. She was going to be in the neighborhood parade.
>
> Johnny wanted to be in the parade, too. And he wanted a balloon on his trike. He had a balloon. But it didn't look like Mary's balloon. It was small and limp.
>
> "Blow it up," said Johnny's brother as he raced out of the house.
>
> How did you do that? Johnny looked at his balloon. Blow it up? What did that mean?

The story would go on from there, showing Johnny approaching a number of family members and getting some piece of advice from each until finally—maybe with some help—he has his balloon on his trike and he proudly enters the parade.

If this were to be for a somewhat older child, the text might be a bit longer and a bit more descriptive.

> Johnny had a new bike. It was a bike, not a trike—though it did have training wheels. It was bright red and Johnny loved it. He wanted everyone to see it. He especially wanted everyone to notice it in the neighborhood parade on the Fourth of July. So he decided he ought to have a big balloon tied to the back. That way everyone would have to look at him in the parade.
>
> "I need a balloon," Johnny said to his mother.
>
> "I think there's one left from your birthday party," his mother told him. "It's in the drawer in the kitchen."
>
> Sure enough, there it was, at the back of the drawer. But it was limp and small. It needed to be blown up. Johnny put

the open end in his mouth and blew. Nothing happened.

Keep the tone and atmosphere of your story consistent. Once you have decided the level at which you will tell your story, follow through to the end at the same level. If you find that the story does not work as you had hoped it would at this level, you may need to rethink the level at which you are writing. Try it simpler, or try it a little more complicated.

You may even find that what you need to do is to think about where you are beginning your story. You may want to try beginning in a different place. As I have said before, one of the great problems with all kinds of manuscripts, but especially picture book manuscripts, is that people don't know where to begin. They want to explain too much at the start. You begin at the beginning, yes. But the beginning is where the real action begins, not with all that happened before. Notice that the examples above begin with action; neither goes into the past. We don't see Johnny getting his bike, or Johnny finding out about the parade. We see Johnny ready to go, except for the balloon.

Once you have decided where to begin, tell the story as compactly as you can, but don't abbreviate so much that it is impossible to tell what is happening, or use short, stubby sentences that do not have a good rhythm. (John has a bike. John and his bike are going to be in a parade. John wants a balloon for the back of his bike.) You may be counting on the illustrator to carry a good deal of the action and the continuity, but even so, your story must read smoothly, and a reader must be able to tell what is happening without the pictures. At the same time, you should tell what you must and no more. Do not get so carried away that you tell too much. *If your typed text runs more than six double-spaced pages, you may no longer have a picture book.*

How long should it take you to write your story? Some people can write all day and at the end have only one page. Others write a whole story in a couple of hours. As we've discussed, minds are different, ideas are different, and no one way of writing is the only right way. Take all the time you need, but don't let yourself putter around getting nowhere. When I write, if I come to a place where I can't seem to think of how the next phrase — or phase — of what I am doing ought to go, I think maybe I have written enough for that day. (Assuming that I have written something.) But I am back at it the next day, and often what seemed impossible the day before is very simple now — my subconscious has worked on the problem in the meantime and solved it. If I am still unsure, however, I write something, even if I think I may want to change it in a rewrite. Actually, I've found that sometimes the parts that come easily are those that most need to be changed in a rewrite, and those that I hammer out with difficulty may be the best of the writing. So no matter what your problems as you write, do not despair. In the end, you will have a story on paper — one that can at least be a basis for rewriting, that will give you a start on what you want to do.

So keep at it, no matter how many problems you encounter. If you don't you may never finish your story or you may lose the thread of it. A first draft of a picture book needs to be completed while your mind is focused on it and you see the story developing in one clear fashion. The King in *Hamlet* said, "That we would do, We should do when we would; for this 'would' changes . . . ." What was true long ago in Denmark is also true about writing a book, any kind of book. We change, and what we put into a book is the solidification of what we are at any given moment. Maybe not tomorrow, maybe not even next week or next month, but soon our lives overtake our ideas and change them. We need to finish what we do while the vision is clear, while the central focus still belongs to the moment in which we are living. For example, you may have decided to write the balloon story because your child or your grandchild had a similar experience. But, especially if it is your child and you live with that child daily, he or she will soon grow past the age where that event is meaningful, and you may have difficulty recreating the child as he or she was.

Finally, before you can call your first draft finished, you must think of a title for your story. Maybe you started with a title and this is no problem. But if you do not have a title, you need one. Think about your story. Think about the main idea, the central focus of what you have done. Can you think of a few words that capture the essence of that focus, without giving away everything that happens in the story? Your title should be one that will attract readers but that will not give them a false idea of what happens in the story. That story about the boy who needed to blow up a balloon might be called *The Reluctant Balloon* or *How John Joined the Parade* or *Balloon Business* or *Blow Up My Balloon*. Which do you like best? Which would you choose? Make a list for yourself of all the possible titles you can think of. Put the list away for a few days, then come back to it. Do any of the titles leap out at you? If not, try thinking of more. Read your list to others; see which title attracts others. You don't have to make a final decision now, but by the time you are ready to send your manuscript to a publisher, you will need that title. So keep at it until you have one that feels right for the book. If the story is eventually accepted for publication, the publisher may, for various reasons, want to change your title (with your permission and approval, of course). But feel comfortable with the one you choose before you give up on your own search.

STEP SEVEN – LET THE FIRST DRAFT MELLOW

When you have finished your first draft, read it over, change what you want to change—correct spellings, change a word here and there, do whatever occurs to you to do—there will always be something that doesn't seem right and obviously needs help. You may want to go back to some of the notes you made to yourself while you were in the thinking stages to see if there are words and phrases and ideas that are not in the finished story but that might belong. If this is the case, put them in, but make sure your patching is seamless—that the new additions seem to have grown where they are from the beginning. For example, if your writing of the balloon story is a simple one designed for quite young children, but in your notes you had a sequence of action that you loved—where Johnny went racing off to find the nice older woman who walks her dog past the house every day, hoping she can help him—and this does not appear in your first draft, you might want to think twice about putting it in. That woman might live too far for a three-year-old to go safely. A five-year-old, maybe, but not a three-year-old. Similarly, if your text is designed for an older child, you will not want to put in language that might best fit the simpler story. You might like the idea of Johnny's brother racing past and simply saying "Blow it up." If it is not in your text, you might decide to put it in. But you cannot have the older Johnny wondering how you blow it up—an older child knows how it is supposed to be done. It is just simply that he can't do it. What is true of action is also true of language. New language must fit the old. Smooth over additions, both language and action, until you hardly know, yourself, what is new and what was old.

When you finish your draft, and when you have made whatever corrections seem necessary, you probably will like what you have done very much. The whole will be surrounded with a bright warm haze of delight and creative pleasure. You will be sure that no one has ever written such a good story before. Though this is the way it may seem to you, this is not likely to be the truth. (Even knowing all this, I find myself thinking something I have done is wonderful when I have just finished it — the truth is something I discover only some time later — it is not as good as it seemed.)

To discover what you have really written, you — and I — need to put the whole thing away for several days, or, better, for several weeks (several months is even better, if you can develop that kind of patience — I can't, I'm afraid).

While the manuscript is put away, think about it from time to time. Make notes to yourself if something new occurs to you that maybe should be a part of the story, or if something occurs to you that you know is there but that maybe does not belong there. Then, one day, take it out, read it over, and see what you have actually written. Ask yourself: Does this story tell me everything I need to know to understand what is happening? Do the plot and the characters and the background work well together — do I come to know and understand them all? Does the language flow well and reinforce the story as it is being told? Is the focus sharp, the action sure, and the resolution of the plot reasonable? You may well find that the story does not fulfill all of your rosy thoughts about it. Information the reader really needs to know is not there; it was in your mind and you thought it was written out, but it was not. The characters, now that they are a bit further from your thinking than they once were, don't seem as well defined as you had imagined. The action does not move in as coordinated a fashion as you had planned. Or any one of a number of problems may have cropped up that you did not anticipate. The story is not what you thought it was.

Do not despair. This happens to all writers, which is why it is a good idea to put a piece of writing away for reconsideration. Now is the time for real revision.

STEP EIGHT — REVISING YOUR MANUSCRIPT

Read your manuscript carefully, looking at it as if you had never seen it before, as if someone else wrote it. What information must be added to make the story clear to a reader? Where should that information appear? If the characters do not seem as real or as well defined as you want, how can you improve the situation — what words in the speech and actions of the characters can be changed to give a sharper image of the person behind those words and actions? If the background does not add the proper dimension and interest to the story, what further part does it need to play in the development of the plot? Do any words call too much attention to themselves? What words would be better? Are there places where you stumble over the rhythm of a sentence, where the pattern of words is awkward? How can those passages be rephrased to sound the way they ought to sound, if they are going to reflect your story well? Go back to the chapter on language. Think again of what you learned there and put that learning to work now to improve your story.

Look at your story first as a whole, then by sections, then by paragraphs and sentences. Analyze what you ought to do. Do not fall in love all over again with what you have done. Instead, be ruthless. Cut where it occurs to you to cut; Somerset Maugham is said to have remarked that in revising his novels if the thought occurred to him to cut something, he cut it; if the thought could occur, the material was not needed. What is true for a novel is surely true of a picture book text. At the same time, it is important to discover places that need to be expanded in order for some aspect of plot or character to be revealed, or to create a smooth transition from one sequence of action to another. Cut, add, do what is necessary to make your story the one you really wanted to write.

Revision, when it comes to the actual doing of it, can be done in a number of ways. You can go through and patch and change and revise and then retype. Or you can simply begin anew, using what you now know about your story and write it again from scratch. You may or may not refer to the first draft as you write. Some writers work one way, and some the other, and some use both methods. Whatever you do, keep a fairly clean copy of your first draft so that you can go back to it and compare it with later versions. Sometimes, in the end, that first version with minor repairs will prove to be better than any later version. Sometimes parts of the first will work well with parts of the second. But when you revise, if you are patching, keep those patches cohesive with the whole — keep the level of diction, the choices of words, the rhythm of speech and presentation consistent. Make it seamless.

Revise, put away, and if necessary revise again. But don't revise forever. Too much revision can deaden a work just as surely as too little revision may leave it unfinished. Revision is a "re-vision" of a work—a way to take another look, to see it in another way, and also to look at it for how well it fulfills the initial vision that inspired it—but it is not a way to make what you have written perfect. There is no such thing as a perfect book—and if there were, it would be dull. It is our flaws as well as our perfections that make us interesting, and what is true of people is also true of stories (within limits, of course).

STEP NINE—TEST WHAT YOU HAVE DONE

There will come a moment when you either believe that there is no more you can do to your story, or you are so tired of it that you can't bear the thought of even reading it again, or you are so confused about what you have and what you don't have that you do not know what to do next. When such a moment comes, the time has arrived for testing what you have done.

The first test is to read the story aloud to yourself. You may be surprised at what reading aloud reveals. And remember, picture books are generally read aloud—that's how they get to their intended audience most of the time. When you read, you will not be reading for plot or character or background, but for the flow of language and of action—for places where big events happen too quickly or where the reading drags. You may find infelicities of phrasing that silent reading may not have revealed, places that are hard to read aloud because the spoken words are cumbersome, places where the sentences and paragraph rhythms do not quite match the action—especially if you are reading with expression and trying to make your voice and pace reflect the action. Your text should almost force a reader into dramatizing a little. If it doesn't, give it a little help. Think about figures of speech, fast and slow words, long sentences and short. Make your text one that reads aloud with expression.

Then comes the second test. Read the text to a friend or relative whose judgment you trust, someone who knows what children like. Or let that person read the story quietly, while you are in another room. Then discuss the work: Did your reader understand the story? Did the reader come to know the characters and see them as you intended they be seen? Did the reader like the story? Did the reader have questions about anything the characters said or did, about the plot as a whole, about the ending? Listen to your reader's ideas and thoughts, then do what you think best with them. You don't have to take any or all opinions you are given. You only need to wonder why the reader had those opinions — and when you understand why, decide if they are valid opinions. Remember that if and when you submit your story to a publisher and again when and if your story becomes a book, readers who do not know you will be evaluating what you have done. If they are likely to see the same problems and ask the same questions as your current reader, it will be too late for you to make changes. So do what you believe is necessary, but do not violate the basic nature of your story just to satisfy the opinions of one friend. You may be as right as the friend — maybe even righter.

At this stage, further tinkering with the story may be small. It is unlikely you will sit down and rewrite the whole again. But do be honest with yourself. Ask for one final time if the story really does work, if it does what you want it to do, if it is the story you set out to tell, and if it is a story worth telling, worth the time of a child and the adult who will read it to the child. It may be hard to decide that what you have done is not really worth further attention, but it is better to decide that now than after you have spent months and maybe even years trying in vain to sell it to a publisher. Better to put your time and efforts on something more likely to succeed.

Chances are, however, that if you have worked carefully and well, you will have a story that is worth sending to an editor.

STEP TEN — GETTING YOUR MANUSCRIPT READY FOR AN EDITOR

No matter how carefully you prepared your manuscript for that final reading, now is the time to make sure you have a perfect copy for an editor to read. Check any questionable spellings. Check all punctuation. Then type the story for a last time if you are using a typewriter, or print it out for a last time if you are using a computer and printer. Make sure that your final version is double-spaced, has adequate margins (at least one inch top and bottom and at the sides as well), that the pages are numbered, preferably at the top right. Put your last name on each page — generally next to the page number — so that it will be clear to which manuscript each page belongs in case there is some sort of mix-up at the publisher.

Unless your story is on your computer and not likely to be lost there, be sure you have one copy to send and at least one copy to keep. Most publishers are very good about keeping track of manuscripts, but once in a great while something does get lost. After all, publishers receive thousands of manuscripts every year, and the staff that handles the manuscripts is likely to be small. Also, it is not unheard of for manuscripts to get lost in the mail. In fact, my recollection is that this happens once or twice a year. So you need to have a copy of the final version of your work.

If your manuscript is very short, put your name and address on the first page. But if your manuscript is more than two or three pages, add a title page that carries the name of the story and your name and address. This is important in case your story should get separated from the stamped self-addressed envelope you are going to include with your mailing.

And now it is time for the great adventure — submitting your story to a publisher. How to go about that is the subject of another skill altogether. You will come to that information in the chapter on marketing — Skill Eight.

Writing a Nonfiction Picture Book

Not too many people think of nonfiction when they think of picture books. It is the story book—the old tale, the modern adventure, the animal adventure, even the realistic animal story—that comes to mind. But actually, nonfiction books are probably as numerous as fiction books. What else would you call an ABC book, a counting book, a familiar item recognition book designed for very young children, or a book about colors? Sometimes, it is true, these learning experiences are couched in story form, but much more often they are simply books of straight nonfiction.

Beyond these quite elementary books are a host of others that are more clearly nonfiction: introductions to nature, to attitudes toward personal relationships, to various kinds of childhood experiences like going to the doctor and dentist or going on a trip to see a distant relative. There are those who try to treat nonfiction like fiction (Uncle John explaining the universe) but children generally prefer their information straight. They like nonfiction. There are hordes of children who prefer books on trucks or dogs or dinosaurs to picture book stories, and they grow restless when a basically meaningless story gets between them and what they want to know. They want to learn. For them, pseudo-fiction that cloaks nonfiction ideas in an unrealistic story is more an annoyance than a help. This does not mean that children cannot be incorporated into a nonfiction text, but simply that there does not have to be a plot or an adult doing the explaining. The book does the necessary explaining.

If you have information you would like to convey to young children, then, do consider writing straight nonfiction. Like all writing for the picture book age child, the kinds of texts required are not easy to write. But for those who have a real bent for nonfiction, they can be easier and more satisfying to write than stories. So, if you believe that nonfiction is the place for you, here are ten steps toward creating a great nonfiction picture book text.

STEP ONE – CHOOSING A SUBJECT

Almost any topic can be the subject of a children's picture book. The main limitations to what can be done are the limited amount of background a child is likely to bring to any subject and the limited attention span that a young child may have. Among the topics that appear frequently and that will certainly appear again and again in children's books are: nature, of course, all phases of nature; animals — dogs, cats, farm animals, wild animals; human beings and how bodies work; the kinds of work adult human beings do — the workers a child is likely to encounter, including community helpers like police and firefighters; other children — many races, many ways of living; what life was like when Mother and Father, Grandmother and Grandfather were children; the alphabet and numbers; simple tools that are used around the house; words, silly and useful, and what they mean; experiences most children have — doctor, dentist, school, city, small town, country, vacations in the mountains or seashores, etc.; vehicles and machines — cars, trucks, buses, trains, airplanes, tractors, earth-moving equipment, etc.; dinosaurs, dinosaurs, dinosaurs; brief biographies of famous people; simple sports; how to do many simple things that children would enjoy. The list can be endless. The subjects that writers probably should avoid are real-life rescues of birds and small animals, preachy books on behavior (funny ones are OK — the ones with exaggerated humor), and books that try too hard to push adult understandings on children.

Children want to know all about the world they live in, and nonfiction is there to explain it to them. It helps them understand the people and activities they see, and lets them know that beyond the scope of their everyday lives there is other knowledge to be acquired. In other words, books of nonfiction can help a child better understand what he already sees and partly knows, and can also take him at least a short distance beyond his present experience. Children like to learn. Learning is a part of being a child.

How do you choose a subject from all of this? You may already know just what you want to write. But if you are not sure — if many things appear possible to you — then think about what appeals to you most. You need to know yourself and your own interests. What do you already know a lot about that you think children would find interesting? Or what topic would you really like an excuse to explore? Writing out of your own knowledge is a perfectly valid way to write. But deciding to educate yourself on a given topic and then writing about it is equally valid. Make a list of all the topics you might choose. Put the list away for a couple of days, then bring it out again. What on the list leaps out at you as being something for which you have real enthusiasm? Then think about children — will children be able to understand this topic? Will there be interest enough in the topic to make it a viable subject? If necessary, do a little research — talk with parents, teachers and librarians to see if there are children who would want to know about your subject. If there does seem to be interest in your proposal, you may have chosen your subject. But there is more to think about before you decide for sure.

First of all, you need to consider the scope of your topic. Some subjects cannot be covered in a 900-page book, let alone a 32- or 40- or even 48-page book. Can your topic, or can some part of it that will make sense in isolation, be covered in an understandable manner — with room for pictures — in the brief space a picture book allows? You can't explore all the trees in the world in one book, but you can get across the idea of what a tree is and the differences between some of the common trees that most children who live in a temperate climate might see. Children could learn that trees have flowers and seeds and leaves or cones and needles. Very young children have a vague concept of time, so telling children that a tree can live for hundreds of years would not mean much. But to say that a tree planted by grandfather, when mother was a child, is now a large shade tree, but that tree will be even bigger when the child is an adult, can mean something.

In other words, nonfiction for the picture book age must take into account the perceptions of the world and the background that the child brings to the book. What may seem like a small topic to an adult may seem like a large topic to a child. An adult may not think that progression from a bud to a full-blown flower to a seed is a whole book, but to a child it may be as much as he or she can comprehend in one volume and may open a whole new view of the out-of-doors. Your topic should be large enough to give a complete picture of something — bud-to-flower-to-seed. At the same time, it should be small enough for a child to understand it all and to be able to grasp what is happening. It must also relate to the child's world. (Dinosaurs may be important to even quite small children, and a nonfiction picture book about a few major varieties of dinosaurs could work very well for small children, even though they might not understand just how long ago dinosaurs lived; on the other hand, a book about Neanderthals would probably leave a child baffled.) Common sense and a certain reasonableness can be a good guide as to what topic you might want to choose.

Next you must consider whether or not your topic will really make a picture book. You have already asked whether or not it would interest a child. But you must also ask yourself whether or not it will use pictures in a useful way. A nonfiction picture book must have pictures that do not simply decorate the page, but that add further information on the topic. Pictures and text must work together to explain the matter. If you cannot imagine how pictures will be able to extend your text and complement it, then you do not have a topic for a picture book. A book about trees can have pictures that show varieties of leaves, varieties of tree shapes, varieties of tree flowers. But a book about how to write a poem — developing rhyme schemes, etc. — would probably be of little interest to a child, who, if he wrote a poem, would do so spontaneously. And pictures probably would not help the subject very much.

If your topic has passed these criteria, take a look at the nonfiction books in your local library. See what else has been done on the topic you have chosen. Don't do what I have seen too many novice nonfiction writers do, choose a subject because it "has never been done." Maybe it has never been done because it should not be done. Think about the idea in terms of children and the society in which they live. Maybe your subject is new and needs to be done, but maybe it is simply too obscure or too limited in appeal to find an audience. At the same time an idea can be overdone. If you want to do a picture book text on dog fleas — their anatomy and their operation on dogs — and you find that sixteen similar books have been published in the past two years, you might want to wait a while before writing your book — until some new research and some new opinions on dog fleas are available.

Finally, ask yourself if the topic is one that you really care about and will continue to care about even after you have worked at it for a long time. If you think that you may become bored by the whole subject, drop it. If you are bored, your readers will be bored, too. To create excitement about a subject in someone else, you must be excited about it yourself.

Even after you have done all of this and have decided on a topic that you think will work for you, you may have more decisions to make. As you think about your topic you may find that it is bigger than you first imagined. You might, for example, have a burning desire to tell every child in the world how marvelous it is to ride a horse. If so, you will, of course, choose to write about riding a horse. But even so limited a topic may not be as limited as it seems. Most children have never ridden a horse. Some may never even have seen a horse. So where do you begin and what do you include? You will, I suspect, begin with the horse: how big it is, how big a child's pony might be. Think of a word, or maybe two or three words at most that will describe the horse—chunky, stolid, frisky, kindly. Do not overdo the adjectives, but you will want to give a child a sense of what a horse is like. Then think about the rider. What does the rider wear—jodhpurs, jeans, boots? How does the rider get on the horse? Where do the rider's feet go? What does the rider sit on? (Do you describe getting the horse ready—putting on the saddle and bridle? Depends on just what your main focus is.) Will the horse move while the rider gets on? How do you get a standing-still horse to start moving? Will the horse run away with you? On what sorts of paths does the horse go? How long will you ride? Who goes along for the ride? All of these things might be a part of a simple picture book. But at the same time, to tell even all of this, not going into any of the techniques of riding, might be too much. You as the author must decide what major information you want a child to get from your book and focus on the material that will convey that information.

You have selected your topic only after you have gotten a clear idea of how much you can tell readers in the book you want to write. It may be that you will need to make outlines for yourself to see how much you can cover. But before you can do this, you may need to do some further research, especially if the topic is one for which you need to gather information before you can begin to write.

STEP TWO — RESEARCHING YOUR IDEA

A nonfiction book for children needs to be accurate. The text may be short, it may be limited, but what it does say and what the pictures show must be completely true. The information the book contains must continue to be true no matter how much more children learn about the subject in later years. Whether what you write is a foundation for later learning or peripheral to it, it must continue to have validity. Of course, sometimes new scholarship changes old knowledge. No one can predict when this might happen. But when you write, the facts must be acceptable at the moment.

This means research. Whatever subject you choose, even if it's one you already know everything about, you should do some research. No matter how much you know — unless you are the world's leading authority — there is almost always something new to know about any given topic. Even in history, which one would think could not change, there are always new views on any given era to be considered. So read as much as you can, talk with experts if you can, absorb as much information as is possible. Make notes to yourself so you will not forget salient points — either on cards that may be filed by topic or in a notebook. Jot down names of especially helpful books so that you can come back to them as needed. Keep track of where you found pictures and charts that might be of help to an illustrator, if your book finds a publisher. Clearly not all of the knowledge you assemble can go into your book, but it is important to know a subject well enough to be able to pick out those areas most suitable for a beginner and to be sure that what you choose fits comfortably into the total body of knowledge. If you read and read and read and talk with one or two experts and still cannot decide where truth lies and what fundamentals of the topic are most accessible to children, then you might want to choose another subject.

Not all subjects demand a great deal of reading, of course. Some require field trips instead. Maybe you decide to write about the U.S. Postal Service. You think, quite correctly, that children like to get letters and they like to draw pictures to send to Grandma and Grandpa. How do those letters and pictures get to the places to which they are sent? Children, you think, might want to know. It might make getting and sending mail even more exciting. But what do you do next?

Unless you are a long-time post office employee and know every aspect of the service—past, present and future—you begin by doing research. You might go first to the library to see what information can be garnered there—and to see, at the same time, just how many post office picture books are already available. (If there are ten, mostly new, think again about your topic.) Read whatever you can find about the post office, but then do your major research: your field trips. Call the local post office—the largest one in your area—and ask to visit. Tell them what you plan to do. Unless it is the Christmas season, they will probably be glad to hear from you. After all, positive publicity for the post office is rare enough that your kind of attention should be welcomed. Visit the post office, talk with the people there, see the kinds of sorting machines they use, discover what the clerks at the windows do, what the mail carriers do, how the mail moves from one city to another, what post office operations most of us never see. Then go home and think about what you have learned. Decide whether or not you need to visit another kind of post office—a local office, or a postal center of some sort.

It may seem foolish to try to learn so much about a topic when so little can be included in a finished book. But it is important for you to write from an abundance of knowledge, rather than to risk making errors simply because you don't know enough. You need to be sure that what you are saying has complete validity.

STEP THREE—FOCUSING YOUR TEXT

When you have completed your research, you assemble all that you have—everything you know that pertains to your subject—and then you must decide just what will go into your text. Ask yourself first: What is the most important point you want to make? Then ask what information a child will need in order to understand that point. What is the simplest bit of information, in other words, where is the beginning point of your book—the place where a child with little background in your subject can best enter the book, the place that comes closest to his own personal experience? What comes next? Build a pyramid of information, each new idea building on what went before, until you reach the top, the understanding you wanted to convey.

Your book should not ramble. It should set a pattern and follow it. It should begin at what you have decided is the beginning—at the easiest information to understand—and move slowly into the more difficult material. It should make each new step of knowledge interesting as well as understandable. The children who come to your book should always know where they have been, understand where they are, and have some idea of where they are going. The ongoing progress of the book from one idea to the next should always be sharp and evident.

For the post office book, for example, you might want to trace a letter and a package from one house to another. Maybe you could suggest that the reader is sending a letter and a package both, the first to a grandparent who lives in another state and the second to a friend who is away. This will not be a story. It will not have a plot. But it will have a structural pattern. It will begin at home—a familiar place—with familiar activities—drawing a picture for grandparents and wrapping a birthday present for a friend. The present will also be wrapped for mailing. Then will come the visit to the post office, the operations of the post office as the letter and the package go on their way. In the end, both letter and package are received and acknowledged.

If you did all of that post office research, you would probably find that not everything you learned would fit into your picture book text. In fact, you would not have done enough research if it did all fit in. You should never be able to tell everything you know in a picture book. You must know enough to know what is important and what can be left out, not because it is not important perhaps, but because it is not necessary to this particular book.

For some, deciding what should go into a book is easy. For others, it is difficult because all of the information gathered is interesting. If you are having trouble deciding what belongs in a book and what does not, try to abstract yourself from the information. Distance yourself from it. Try to imagine yourself as a newcomer to this knowledge. This will be most difficult for you if you are the world's leading expert in the field. It will be easiest if you have just studied the area for the first time. In either case, you may have trouble letting go of interesting facts that nevertheless don't belong. Yet, consider your reader. How much will the child who encounters that post office book really want to know? How to mail a letter and a package; where they both go — in general terms but including some sorting and some travel on planes, etc., and how they are delivered? You will not talk about how the post office sorting machines were developed or even exactly how they work, probably. That they exist may be enough.

If you have made notes to yourself, go through them, circle the items that pertain directly to that major point you want to make. If you have not made notes before, make them now. Make lists of the information you think might be a part of the book. Then go through and circle those that you are sure must be a part of the book. Try to think of the pattern they ought to take, of where the material should begin, how your pyramid of information should be built, what the apex of that pyramid will be, and how you will summarize the whole at the end.

Some books, however, may not need this kind of progression. If you are writing a picture book on different kinds of tree leaves, for example, you will organize your material in a different way. The idea you are probably trying to get across is that leaves are not all the same. For young children it may be enough to say first that not all tree leaves are alike. Then you could explain that some leaves are big — catalpa — some leaves are small — hawthorn — some leaves are single — maple — some leaves come in groups or have many little parts to one leaf — ailanthus — etc. Or you might want to become a bit more scientific and categorize leaves by some other designation. What you are trying to do, however, is show variety, and at the end some sort of summary will be needed to bring together all of the different kinds of leaves presented. Here, instead of a pyramid supporting the main idea, you have a cluster, a series of columns holding up a roof (a Parthenon rather than a pyramid).

Think about your aim, about the kind of information you want to convey, and then decide how much supporting information is needed to make your final conclusion understandable. Discard all other information, no matter how interesting it is.

STEP FOUR — THINK ABOUT PICTURES

As you plan what will go into your book, do not forget that there will be pictures. Pictures will help you keep your text short and to the point. You will not need to go into lengthy descriptions of physical elements involved in your text because the pictures will show them. Furthermore, as with all kinds of picture books, when you select the pieces of information needed to build your pyramid or your Parthenon, you should select those that will permit an artist to extend your text with pictures and that will allow good picture variety.

If you were writing the post office book, you would not need to describe the machines that the post office uses. The pictures would show them. You wouldn't have to describe post office trucks. Pictures would show them. What you would have to present is the thread of progress as the items make their way from one place to another. The letter and package would go from the child into the post box, or, in the case of the package, into the hands of a postal clerk. Then letter and package would slowly make their way—be sorted, bagged, carried by plane, unsorted, put into a delivery truck or whatever—and finally arrive at their destinations.

For the tree book, you might want to state the basic group to which each kind of leaf belongs, but the picture will show how each leaf looks.

As you did research, it was suggested that you keep notes of books and other materials an artist might want to use as a resource for the illustrations. Check to see what you have, what items it will be easiest for the artist to picture—this may come into your planning as you try to decide what to put into the book and what not to put there. If you visit places as part of your research, you may want to take photographs for an illustrator to use as reference. In fiction there is room for interpretation by an artist; that is not so true in nonfiction, where the artist must be accurate and represent your text faithfully. The information you make available can be very helpful, as can your very careful planning to allow text and pictures to work together to make a cohesive whole.

STEP FIVE—MAKE AN OUTLINE

You may have made many outlines of what you plan to do before you get to this stage. But now is the time to make a final outline. Review all that you have done; consider again, in light of material that must be a part of your book and material that will lend itself well to illustration, the pattern your book ought to take. Keep in mind that the pictures ought to be spaced evenly through the book. Then organize the way you will present your text.

Most picture books contain 32 pages, of which 28 are generally given over to text and illustration. The remaining pages are for title page, copyright, dedication, etc. Your outline should take this into consideration. But first, organize your pyramid or your Parthenon on the basis of the facts that must be presented.

If you are writing the post office book, you might begin an outline in this fashion:

I. Origination of mail
   A. child or children preparing pictures or letter
   B. wrapping of package

II. Mailing of pieces
   A. dropping letter into post box
   B. giving package to postal clerk

III. Postal pick-up at the post box

IV. Sorting at the post office
   A. letter
   B. package

V. Various operations from there on to delivery (you would probably spell these out more completely)

This might break down into pages as follows (no matter how many pages of front matter a book has, the first page of text is almost always a right hand page, and it is often numbered page 3):

Page 3 — children making pictures and letter
Page 4 — wrapping package
Page 5 — walking to post box and dropping letter
Page 6 — at the post office window
Page 7 — pick-up at the post box — and delivery to post office
Pages 8 and 9 — sorting of mail and packages at local post office

It may take quite a while to get a satisfactory outline and breakdown into prospective pages, one that will give the basic information needed, give the right amount of space to each aspect of the matter, and allow reasonable spacing for pictures. Whatever time this takes is worth spending, because in nonfiction the pattern of ideas, the progression of ideas, and clarity of purpose and meaning are all important. Of course, the writing style in which all of this is conveyed is the factor that will eventually determine how effective the manuscript is, but no matter how good the writing, if the material is not well organized, the result will be a book that does not accomplish what you intend.

As you outline, and as you plan pages, try to keep yourself abstracted from the whole, keep your eye on the end to which you are moving, make sure that each page will contain information of interest and will strengthen your conclusion. Test each element you include. Skip it and see if you find it hard to move from the one before to the one after without it; if it is not necessary, eliminate it; if it is needed, keep it. Continually test your progression of information. If any one item requires too much explanation, you may need another step. Make the steps of your pyramid even; make the columns of your Parthenon equal.

STEP SIX—WRITING A FIRST DRAFT

Now at last you are ready to write your text. You have an outline that tells you just how much of what you know is going to be a part of your manuscript and the order in which that information is going to be presented. Probably by now you have a good idea of what age group you are addressing. If not, now is certainly the time to decide. You can't decide any later. The age group for which you are writing will determine how long a text you ought to have and how complicated your presentation can be. A book for two-year-olds will stick to the basics of the everyday world the child is likely to see all the time; for three-year-olds, you can venture a little further afield—into simple excursions into nature, into relationships with siblings and other relatives, into the community and the people who can be encountered there; for four-year-olds, you can begin to explore nature more deeply, take vacations, and enter into activities of nursery school; five- and six-year-olds are almost ready to read and certainly know a good deal of the world from TV—they are ready for almost anything you can give them, if you present it in the gradual steps needed for all picture books. You need not decide exactly what age child your book is for but you need to remember that not all picture books need to be for all children, and that a very young subject—the basics of everyday life in a limited scope—demands a young approach — short sentences and short texts for short attention spans.

You must make one other decision as you begin to write: the overall tone your work will take. Much of this depends on your subject, but any subject can be treated in several ways, depending on the age child for whom you intend your book, and the feeling you want readers to take from your book.

If you are writing the text for an ABC book featuring fruit for a two-year-old, you might simply list *Apple, Banana, Cantaloupe, Date, Elderberry*, etc. For a three-year-old — when nonsense is beginning to be important — the simple words might be embroidered a bit (remember that verse and poetry are, technically, nonfiction): *Apple, Appley, Apple sauce/ Banana split, Banana toss/ Cantaloupe seed and Cantaloupe ball/ When do Dates on Date trees fall? /* etc. (Do not think that this is an ideal approach — simply an example. Don't try verse or poetry unless you have read the chapter on poetry and verse and are ready to tackle its difficulties.) For four- and five-year-olds, one might go into a little more detail on those fruits, describing them, perhaps, in some imaginative way that will make clear what a child can expect from consuming each or even describing how and where they grow to show that the fruits we eat come from different countries and different climates.

If you are writing the post office book for three- or four-year-olds, the text for each page will probably be quite simple, but will tell enough to give the child an understanding of what is happening. The text for pages 3 and 4 of the outline might read:

> Suppose you drew a picture one day and you wanted your grandmother to have it. What would you do if your grandmother lived far away? Your mother would probably say that you could mail it to your grandmother.
>
> Or maybe you had a friend who had moved to another city. How could you send him a birthday present? Your mother would probably say you could send it by mail.
>
> You would put your picture in an addressed and stamped envelope, and you and your mother would go to the post office. You would drop it in a slot and it would be on its way to your grandmother.
>
> But you and your mother would have to take your package to the post office counter.

This is all you would have to say for younger children on those first pages, and the remaining pages would be just as simple, in general content. If, however, you were writing this book for five- and six-year-olds, you might want to go into greater detail. Such a book might begin like this:

If you had a grandmother who lived far away and you wanted to tell her something, you might call her on the telephone. But if you had drawn a very special picture for her, with lots of different colors, you couldn't send that over the telephone, not even if you had a fax machine. So you would mail it to her. And if you had a package you wanted to send to a friend who lives in another city, you might also send that by mail. The post office takes all kinds of mail from people everywhere and sends it wherever those people want it to go.

This version would go on from there in much the same vein, giving just a little more information on each page and bringing in a bit more of the world of today that surrounds the child.

Once you have decided who your audience is and how much information you want to convey, you must decide on the overall tone of your work. Will it be nonsense like the fruit ABC verse? Will it be direct and informative, simply stating facts? *(Trees are everywhere, and every tree has leaves of one sort or another.)* Will it, even though it is nonfiction, take on a sort of story-telling quality? *(When you walk through a park, you see trees all around. At first you think they are all alike. But when you begin to look at them, you see that they are different from each other.)* Will it be casual? *(I like trees, don't you? Everywhere I go, I see trees, and I never saw a tree I didn't like. But I do see that they are not all the same.)* Or will it be formal? *(Trees live in almost every part of the world. Wherever people live, trees live. But those trees are not all alike.)* Will it try to involve readers in what is being presented? *(Do you have trees near where you live? They all have leaves, don't they? Have you ever looked at those leaves? If it is summer and the leaves are out, go outside and pick a leaf from two or three trees. Are they the same?)* These are a few of the approaches you might take to the same subject. Think about your material. Which approach will best suit it? Which will allow you to convey the most information most easily? Which do you think will interest and involve children the most easily?

Think a little further. If you are writing a text on the life cycle of the mosquito, do you want to send your readers out to do research? Probably not. Most people don't want to encounter any more mosquitoes than necessary. A direct approach may be a better one for this book. On the other hand, if you are trying to describe how children live in Ghana, you may very well want to use a more involving approach (though not Uncle John taking Les and Jennifer to visit relatives in Ghana — that should be a story, not a nonfiction book) by introducing children who live in various parts of Ghana and describing their lives and activities. Here you might even want to suggest that readers try playing some of the games that children of Ghana enjoy.

The mosquito book and the Ghana book would be for five- and six-year-olds because they require more background of knowledge than most children younger than that are likely to have. But the same approaches apply to books for younger children. A book about a common tree and what happens to it around the year — leafing in the spring, bird's nest in the summer, shade in the summer, colorful in the fall, covered with snow in the winter — could have a very factual approach, or it could have a more story-telling approach — though in nonfiction, not by giving it a name and a personality. *(In the spring, maple trees get new leaves.* Versus: *Spring is the time when all of the outdoors changes. And trees are a part of that change. They get new leaves.)*

When you have decided just what your approach should be, then it is time to put down in some fashion — pencil and paper, computer disk, or whatever — the text as you think it should be. With a nonfiction book, it is generally best to begin at the beginning. Your first sentence should introduce the subject in a general way; it should prepare the reader for what is to come. Write it slowly and carefully. That first sentence is the key to all that will follow: to the tone of the work, the level of the language, the manner in which the subject will be covered. From the first sentence, go on to complete the first paragraph. By the end of that paragraph, your reader should know what the book is going to cover. What follows will be the examples, the development of your thesis, your pyramid steps or Parthenon pillars. And finally at the very end will come a sort of summary of what you have said, something that will reinforce the information you have conveyed and that may even make the reader want to know more.

When you have finished the text for the first page, see if you have said what needs to be said in few enough words and sentences to allow room for a picture. If not, you may need to go back and revise your outline and page breakdown. If the first page works, try the second. See if it works as well. If it does, your earlier work has been well done and you are on your way. If not, you need to do some rethinking.

As you write, you will want to create sentences that have variety, that have rhythm. Nonfiction needs to be as well written as fiction. Look again at the first post office example—on page 87. Would the following do as well?

> One day you drew a picture. You wanted your grandmother to see it. Your grandmother lives far away.
>
> "Send that picture to your grandmother," said your mother. "Send it by mail to your grandmother."

Unless you were writing a particularly dull first-grade reader, that text would not work. The example on page 87 may not be great prose, but it does have rhythm. It is not a series of short, stubby sentences.

You need to put words together in interesting ways that underlie and strengthen the meaning of what you are saying. When the post office book goes to the post office, you could say simply, "The letter must be put into the slot. When you do that it falls into a pile of letters on the other side." Or you could say, "You may have to reach up, but you should slip your letter into the slot, and it will slide down into a pile with other letters that have been mailed." The second version is more personal and uses words that catch some of the action of the event. Both versions, however, are simple and clear, as writing for children must be. You will want to read each of your sentences to see if they give a feeling for the action that is taking place and yet convey that action in a direct and purposeful manner. Of course, the younger the audience you anticipate, the simpler the presentation must be. (For younger children: "Your mother will help you find the right slot for your letter. Stand on tiptoe and let your letter slide in." For older children: "At the post office there will be more than one slot for mail. Your mother will know which is the right one for your letter. Reach up and let your letter slide in. Hear it thump down on the other side.")

Make every word and every sentence count and every word and every sentence build upon or add to the sentence that went before. Use vivid action verbs whenever you can to make your text come alive (*slide in* not *put in*). Choose nouns and modifiers carefully so that the text as well as the illustrations will create pictures in the mind of the reader. Keep the text flowing smoothly. Even if you have planned how the pages will fall, do not write your text as if you were dealing with separate pages. Instead, paragraph, but keep your text together, so you can read it comfortably as a whole and see if there are places where understandings do not bridge over from one sentence to the next, from one paragraph to the next. Of course, in many cases, pictures will carry much of the information that is to be conveyed. Even so, the text needs to flow and to make sense in itself.

Put all of your skills as a writer into what you write. Sentence must lead into sentence, paragraph into paragraph in a logical and interesting fashion. The reader should be more aware of meaning, as the text flows along, than of words. You will probably need transition sentences between one idea and the next to make relationships between ideas clear. Think about those relationships so that they are clear to you. Then put them down in the most direct, understandable way possible. Begin with the idea the child has already grasped and then show how that idea can grow into something that begins the next idea.

> In addition to flat leaves that are big, small, and combinations of little leaves, there is another kind of leaf that you may never have thought of as a leaf. This kind of leaf is called a needle. . . .

Although simplicity and directness and using the fewest words possible is the ideal, remember, especially when you create transitions, that sometimes it is possible to be too cryptic — you need to say enough to make your meaning clear, but no more.

You may sometimes need to use a word that children may not know. If so, put it into a context that will make the meaning apparent, even if you know a parent will be reading the book to the child and can explain. Children love to discover new things for themselves and to work out meanings on their own. If you do use a difficult word, use it more than once, if you can, so that it will be reinforced in a child's mind and become a part of his or her vocabulary. Children like long words, euphonious words, words that trip off the tongue in strange ways. But a text that contains too many difficult words will simply leave a child perplexed. So use them if you must, but don't use them just to use them, and don't use more than a few in an entire book. Too much of even a good thing is too much. Too many strange words can make a book a puzzle rather than an explanation of something interesting.

Your summary at the end should be brief, but useful. It should be both an end and a beginning. That book about trees having different kinds of leaves might end—depending, of course, on the overall tone you choose:

> Leaves are everywhere. Everywhere you go there will be trees, and all of those trees will have leaves. Some will be like the ones you have seen in this book, and some will be quite different. No one knows how many different kinds of leaves there are in the world, but everyone can keep looking to find leaves they have never seen before.

Or you might say:

> There are four main kinds of leaves. But each main kind of leaf can be big or small, fat or thin. Every kind of tree has its own shape of leaf. Knowing the shape of a leaf can help you know the kind of tree on which it grew. Many people like this kind of knowing.

STEP SEVEN — REVISE

You have it down on paper. You think it works. It says something to you. But will it say to others what it says to you? Put your manuscript away for a couple of days. Take a rest. You deserve it. You've been working hard—deciding what you were going to write, doing all that research, establishing the level of your text, outlining, getting it all down in a reasonable form. Writing is hard work. So read a novel. Go to the beach. Ride a horse. Knit a sweater. Do something you enjoy to get your mind off of what you have been doing.

Then in a few days, or a week or so—longer if you can bear

to wait—come back to your manuscript. Evaluate it for yourself, now that your mind has been busy with other things. Look at it as a whole. Does the beginning set the tone, and does that tone follow through? Do ideas follow each other in a logical progression? Can you now see that segments of your text do not belong there and should be cut out? In some places do you need to say a bit more to make yourself understood? Are your transitions from one idea to the next true bridges from one passage to another, carrying the reader from one idea to the next? Does your summary at the end convey the essence of the whole and the thought that for those really interested there is more to be learned? Will the child who encounters your book be able to follow what you have done and maybe even get excited about the ideas you have presented?

Now take a look at the more basic parts of your text. What about your paragraphs? Do they hold together as proper paragraphs? Does each one work as a unit to present one important idea that then leads to the idea to be found in the next paragraph? Do you need all your paragraphs to say what you want to say? And what about your sentences? Are they varied and interesting? Do they each say what you meant them to say? Do they flow from one to the next in a good rhythmic style? Are all of your sentences needed? Could some come out and never be missed? Or do some sentences need more work to make them more complete?

Evaluate your work carefully. And revise what seems to need revision. Revision can be fun. You can think of what you have done, try other ways of doing it, experiment with other words in some places, with new ways of putting sentences and paragraphs together, and most of all you can cut. You can discover that brevity truly is the "soul of wit." But before you begin to work on your manuscript, make sure you keep a clean copy of the first version. In the end, you may find that much of what you did in the beginning was right. So don't lose that first draft. But play with it, try out anything that occurs to you to try, so that when you finish revising, you are sure that what you have is what you really want to have, that your text does, as far as you can determine, exactly what you set out to do.

When you are content with your revisions, type or print out a clean copy of this new version.

STEP EIGHT – LET OTHERS SEE WHAT YOU HAVE DONE

If you have trusted friends whose opinions on your writing you cherish, let them see your work after you revise. Let them point to places that do not quite convey the meaning you had hoped was there. After all, remember, you know a lot about this subject, more than you have put into this book. And there may still be places where what you know gets in the way of your realizing what is and what is not down in the text. Take the comments of your reader, evaluate them in terms of what you intended to do, and use them to improve what you have done. You do not, however, have to alter your style or change the whole of what you are doing to satisfy a reader. Keep the book yours, but yours with whatever revisions may seem needed.

You may want to read the material aloud to yourself, or to others. Often reading aloud makes a writer aware of infelicities of word use, sentences that are awkward, and even meanings that are not clear. Remember that your picture book text will probably be read aloud to the children for whom it is intended. So how well it reads aloud is important.

Finally, if this is a subject about which you are enthusiastic but for which you are not the world's leading authority, you may want to have an expert read what you have written to make sure you have not given your readers a mistaken impression somewhere. If you are writing about the life cycle of a mosquito, a high-school or college biology teacher may be the expert you need. If you are writing about the post office, ask the superintendent of your local post office to read your manuscript. Generally a picture book text does not need to be read by an authority in the field; just someone who knows a lot about the subject will do, someone who can tell you if you have made a disastrous mistake. Do not, however, let this expert reader – or any reader – convince you that you need to rewrite the manuscript in the fashion he or she would have done it. The manuscript is yours and should reflect your ideas and your writing style. All you need from the expert is an evaluation of accuracy. And, if you are writing about something that is controversial, be careful – try to get an expert who agrees with the approach you have taken, though certainly in a case like this, even for young children, you want to indicate that there are differing views.

When you have evaluated the various responses from those who have read your book, you are ready to revise again, maybe.

STEP NINE—REVISE AGAIN?

Take yet another look at what you have done. How have the opinions of others changed your work? Have revisions you have made because of suggestions you have received altered the patterns of paragraphs, altered the rhythm and clarity of sentences? If so, you will need to do some smoothing over. You may even need to rethink whole passages to make them flow naturally. Read the work aloud, make necessary changes until it is impossible to tell that changes have been made.

Now take a final look. Chip away an adverb here, an adjective there, words that suddenly seem unneccessary or out of place. Add a word, perhaps, to improve the rhythm or clarify a meaning. Change a word to get a little closer to complete accuracy somewhere else. Make the whole the total unit you want it to be, the exciting book that will capture the imaginations of hundreds of children and let them see what you saw in the subject you chose.

STEP TEN—GETTING YOUR MANUSCRIPT READY FOR AN EDITOR

Your manuscript is now at a point where the next person who ought to see it is an editor. More in a later chapter about who that editor ought to be, but first make sure that your manuscript is presentable—that it looks professional and will make a good impression on whatever editor receives it.

First of all—type the manuscript, on one side of the sheet, double-spaced, or even triple-spaced, if you think that looks better. Picture suggestions are not needed for fiction, but for a nonfiction book, picture suggestions can help. You need not provide pictures, but you should indicate where a picture is needed and what that picture should be. These picture suggestions can be included in parentheses, before or after each segment of text, or your text can be typed in a narrow column with the picture suggestions next to the text they illustrate.

If you have material that will help the editor see what you see, this can be included with your typed material. You need not make a dummy or paste up pages. You need not draw any kinds of pictures yourself. But if you can give the editor the idea that you can be of help to whoever will do the pictures, passing on research materials or the names of books from which you have gotten information, this may be all to the good. And if what the book will need is not drawn pictures but photographs of material from archives of some sort, if you can indicate that you know sources for these and would even be willing to do the research needed to get that material, an editor may be grateful.

There is no need for you to spend money gathering material of this sort, even when you know it will be needed. Wait until you have a publisher for the work before you make serious attempts to get picture material, and do it then only if the publisher wants you to do it. But do indicate that you can and will be willing to spend time gathering materials if your help is needed. And remember that whatever you suggest must be for illustration that will be done on a professional level. You should not suggest that you will take pictures yourself—at least not pictures that will go into the book, although pictures to be used by an artist for copy may be all right. You can take your own pictures if you are a professional photographer, or do your own drawings if you have professional training as an illustrator, but remember that whatever is to be done must be done in a way that will make the most attractive and accurate book possible.

Do not think, however, that you must send picture suggestions or volunteer to do research for the pictures that will appear in your book. Publishers and illustrators are quite capable of doing this on their own, and often prefer to do so. But when you believe that you have special material or can approach special sources that will make the book all you want it to be, in the case of nonfiction it is not wrong to make suggestions.

Your manuscript is ready to go. Read it over. Are you still pleased with it? Is there some final change you think you would like to make? Don't do it! Tomorrow you will prefer it the way it is. There is a time to revise and a time to stop revising. If an editor takes your book, he or she may suggest further revisions, but until then, or until ten or twelve editors have turned down what you have done, let it go. Forget about it, except to send it off. Begin writing something new. One book is done—at least until someone wants to publish it—and it is time to move on.

Writing Poetry and Verse for Children

Few people believe they can write poetry like Shakespeare or even Emily Dickinson. But almost everyone thinks that verses like those of Edward Lear or Dr. Seuss are simple to do and can be easily tossed off, especially when one is writing for children. Many people also think that children's picture books—fiction, nonfiction, whatever—must come in verse to be acceptable, and the cuter the verse the better.

It is certainly true that almost none of us is Shakespeare or Emily Dickinson. But it is also a fact that almost none of us is Edward Lear or Dr. Seuss. And it is not true that a good children's book must be in verse. In fact, quite the opposite. When a manuscript reader in a children's book department comes upon a manuscript in verse, the reader's first thought is that the manuscript is going to be terrible. The general belief in children's publishing is that only those writers who know nothing about children's books write manuscripts in verse.

Even so, it must be said that children do like verse and poetry, and verse and poetry do get published. The writers are people who know what to write and how to do it successfully.

Picture books feature verse and poetry in a number of ways: as a variety of separate verses or poems, perhaps with a central theme; as stories told in verse (yes, it can be done, but it must be done well); even, in the case of alphabet and number books, nonfiction in verse. The key to writing successful poetry and verse for children is understanding that it is not simply meter and rhyme that must be considered, but pattern and content as well. Writing verse and poetry can be fun and exciting for writers who know how to do it, and who do it well. For those who want to try, here are ten steps that may be helpful.

STEP ONE—DISCOVER THE NATURE OF VERSE AND POETRY

Poetry and verse are often used as interchangeable words for texts that offer, through some sort of patterned use of words, an insight into some aspect of the human condition. They are ways of condensing ideas and thoughts and sometimes stories into tight little packages, where the pattern, the form of expression, is as important to the reader's grasp of meaning as are the words used. Verse generally is thought of as having rhyme and meter and as dealing with ideas that are lighter and more casual than poetry. Poetry is thought of as maybe, but not necessarily, having rhyme, always having a meter of some sort, and being, in a sense, a metaphor, using one experience to represent a larger truth. In other words, verse deals with surface events and poetry deals with ideas that stem from the depths of human experience. Poetry may even tell a story; it can be fun and funny, but it expresses ideas and emotions that readers can reflect upon and say, "Yes, I've felt like that," or "Oh, is that how life is? I see it now."

You don't need to draw the distinction for yourself, probably, but if you plan to write a collection of poetry or verse, you need to keep the tone somewhat consistent.

John's new sled
Was big and red.
"I can," he said,
"Go fast as Ned."
But as they sped,
Ned missed the shed.
Not John!
He bumped his head,
His poor nose bled,
And now in bed
Likes slow instead.

The above is clearly verse—not very good verse, even didactic verse (a real no-no unless you are Dr. Seuss)—and would not belong in the same book with the following:

My sled and I, when snowtime comes,
Skim swiftly down the icy slopes.
"Speed on, speed on, speed on," I cry.
I love this flight on ice and snow.
My kite and I when springtime comes
Go running, running, and it soars;
It flies on high, while down below
I watch and wonder, could I ride?

This is closer to poetry because it sets up a tension between two kinds of experience and raises questions about the relationship between them. It comes from inside the writer, not from an outside observer. It is, in a way, a simple exploration of human limitations. It does not attempt to solve an age-old problem, but merely presents it once again—the contrast between what we can do and we cannot do, the sharpness of longing for something more.

Verse then, often—even generally—presents an open and shut case, an event, an idea that is self-limited. Poetry, on the other hand, opens a thought but does not close it—instead leads the reader on to other ideas and bigger thoughts. Verse is complete in itself; it is exactly what it seems to be; poetry encapsulates in a small image the idea of something much larger.

Which you choose to do depends on what you have to say and how you choose to say it. Remember that both poetry and verse are condensed forms of expression. They exist because they say better than prose what the writer wants to say, and say it in a memorable and concise fashion. When you think you want to write poetry or verse, think about what the content will be. Ask yourself if prose would do as well. If it will, then prose is what you should be writing. Choose verse and poetry only when you are totally convinced that no other form of writing will serve your purpose.

STEP TWO—SEARCH FOR THE EXPERIENCES, IMAGINATION AND EMOTIONS OF CHILDHOOD

More than any other kind of writing for children, poetry and verse demand that the writer understand what it is like to be a child. You will not be able to write poetry and verse that will really speak to a child unless you can think as a child thinks and see the world as a child sees it. This comes not only from observing children—though that certainly does help—but comes, even more, from seeking out and finding the child within you. As was discussed in the first chapter, Skill One, all of us have deep inside the child we once were. Finding that child and writing out of the memory and the persona of that child is not being childish but discovering the childlikeness needed to be a successful writer and especially a successful poet for children.

How does one achieve childlikeness? The basis is the same for all kinds of writing, but again, it is especially relevant for poetry and verse. First of all, observe children. See how they react to a given situation. Compare their reaction to yours. Ask yourself if you are seeing the world around you with the same wonder, the same freshness that a child does. Does an event or a scene or a kind of person that is very familiar still seem worth your exploration—can you see these new, as you once did, even though they have been familiar for years? Poets, whether writing for children or adults, never quite lose the childlike ability to see the everyday as something fresh and original and a beckoning adventure.

Then remember yourself as a child. Can you recall the pride you felt when you first learned to tie a bow? Is not that pride equal to the pride you have felt in adult achievements? Think of other things that delighted you as a child. Remember the things you looked forward to, the things you hated. Then think about how you might interpret those feelings for children of today. What are the current equivalents of the experiences of your childhood? What would children of today like to see expressed for them, based on what you might have liked to read?

It is important that you, the writer, take seriously the attitudes of children, that your poetry and verse for children interpret for them their feelings, their joys and their sadness, in ways that see these things as they see them, that do not disparage their attitudes. You must learn to view life through their eyes, see life from a child's point of view. In fact, you should hold events under a microscope and magnify them so the child can see that others believe his or her actions, feelings and observations are important. If you can put into words the thoughts children have had but have been unable to express for themselves, or put together ideas that have lingered in the child's mind but have not been connected for her or him before, you will have succeeded as a poet and as a person who has discovered the meaning of childlikeness.

Seeking and finding the child within is not easy for most people. A few have never lost it. But for others it can be a journey into the self that is difficult and sometimes even painful. Yet not to do this is to write down to a child—to speak to childhood as an adult sees it and not as a child sees it. The result can too often be coy or cute or overly whimsical or didactic. Children may read such poetry and verse, but they will not return to it. The poems and the verses they love are those that interpret for them the world as they see it.

STEP THREE—UNDERSTAND THE TRADITIONAL STRUCTURE OF VERSE AND POETRY

Verse is more likely to be heavily structured rhythmically and to rhyme than poetry. But all poetry and verse has some sort of rhythm and most verse rhymes. In the past, all poetry and verse was heavily structured and rhymed. But in recent years that has changed. However, you do need to learn the traditional forms, even if you intend to write what is called "free verse."

The traditional rhythms of verse and poetry are divided into categories, and most of us learned them at school. Each line of verse is made up of a given number of "feet," and each foot has both accented and unaccented syllables within it in a given pattern. Just as a refresher, here are the main kinds of feet, where x is an unaccented syllable and * is an accented one:

1. Iambic (x *)—can be a bit singsongish if used too consistently, but a very common foot:

    x   * x   *   x   *   x   *
The *moon* is *white*/The *stars* are *bright.*

2. Trochaic (* x)—a highly emphatic form:

    *   x   *   x   *   x   *   x
Fight on, *fight* on/*Weep* not, *hope* yet.

3. Anapestic (x x *)—often used to convey swift movement:

    x x *   x x *   x   x   *   x   x   *
To a*rise,* to a*rise*/is to *mea*sure the *skies.*

4. Dactylic (* x x)—can be a bit singsongish, but also gives a feeling of rapid movement:

<pre>
  * X X *   X   X * X X   * XX
</pre>
*Child*ren a*woke* to the/*cry* of the *vir*eo.

5. Spondaic (* *)—hard to do with words of more than one syllable—not too many words have the accent on every syllable:

<pre>
   *   *   *   *   *   *   *   *
</pre>
Hold strong good friend/Time does hearts mend.

Beat out the patterns of these feet for yourself. Come to know them. Think of words that fit each pattern. Then think of groups of words that repeat a pattern more than once. Experiment with how the rhythms these feet create add meaning to the words that fall into the various patterns. Then think about line length. Each line of verse contains a given number of feet.

> two feet—a dimeter line
> three feet—a trimeter line
> four feet—a tetrameter line
> five feet—a pentameter line
> six feet—an Alexandrine

Few verses or poems for children will contain lines of more than six feet. Generally each foot in a line of a verse or a poem follows the same pattern—iambic, trochaic, or whatever seems to fit the subject best. However, an extra syllable may be added at the beginning or the end of a line when necessary, or an unaccented syllable at the end of a line can be dropped.

The lines in a complete verse will also generally follow some set pattern. A four-line verse might, for example, begin with an iambic tetrameter, follow that with an iambic trimeter, then another tetrameter and another trimeter. Or a series of six lines might have five trimeters and end with an unexpected pentameter. The form you choose for your verse will determine to some extent how your verse will be interpreted. Short lines, tripping rhythms will give a sprightly air to verse, even if the subject is heavy and serious. Long lines and weighty rhythms will make even light subjects seem heavy. When you have come to know the different kinds of feet well, to understand the rhythms they present, then you will be ready to choose what will best fit your subject matter. Don't opt always for the easiest. Too many people writing verse use iambic in trimeters or tetrameters when something else would be better. Think of the words you most need to use in your verse, and also the subtle meanings you need your rhythms to convey. Here for example are a couple of lines of spondees — would iambic work as well?

> Blow, blow, blow, do blow, Joe, blow.
> We here know that horn says, "Go!"

(Note that all of those words are one-syllable words, again about the only way you will get complete spondaic lines.) To me those lines say that Joe can blow a loud note, one that is enough to start a race of some sort, but I suspect that Joe isn't much when it comes to melody. He is a one-note Joe. Those are one-note lines. Study verse forms, think about them, and get a feeling for what they do.

Most verse rhymes. Much poetry does not. Neither has to rhyme, but children find rhyme fun when it is well used, when it is suitable and sometimes unexpected. Rhymes, like meter, should be carefully planned. Rhyming words should fit the subject: heavy words, long and full of *m*s and *w*s belong in places where a sense of slowness, sadness or difficulty is being presented; silly, flighty words with lots of *l*s and *f*s and *y*s belong in lighter verse because they help to convey fun and nonsense. What is true of rhyming words, is, of course, also true for all the words you use in your verse or your poem. But since the rhymes are the words that people will most look at or "hear" and remember, they must be of first consideration. You may have a perfect line for a poem, but it falls in a place where you need something to rhyme with it. Do not use a word for that rhyme just because it does rhyme, even if you can make the actual meaning fit, if the word does not convey the right spirit as well as the right meaning. If necessary, rewrite your perfect line to bring its rhyme and the succeeding rhyme into harmony of spirit. Here are two versions of the same idea. Which best expresses with rhyme and meter the idea being presented? When rhyme and meter work together well, the writer's feeling is almost transparent.

> Spring is just around the bend,
> That is what the bees portend.

Or:

Spring is coming
Bees are humming

The first is stiff and does not give the feeling of lift that the idea of spring should convey. The second takes off and makes you feel that spring really is on the way, even though the rhyming words are full of those heavy *m*s — the use of trochaic dimeters gives the lines the pace they need. *Coming* and *humming* have a feeling of action that *bend* and *portend* do not.

When writing even the simplest, most mundane verse, let alone poetry, words must fall into acceptable and usual patterns of speech. It does not do to say "I to my grandma's went" just because you want the last word of the line to rhyme with *bent*. You can say "I to my grandma's went" if the emphasis is on *went*, however. If you didn't want to go and were made to go, for example, then the word order might be acceptable. But meaning comes first. If you were writing prose, you might use the same construction for the same reason. In other words, the skill of the versifier is in creating lines that follow metric patterns and use rhyme when wanted and still place words in a word order that seems uncontorted and makes the meaning clear.

As you study the writing of poetry and verse, learn not only how to create patterns of meter and rhyme, but also how to vary meter and rhyme so a poem does not grow dull and singsongish. When you choose the pattern for your work, work out some way of handling what you do so there will be change in the pattern, sometimes as a surprise, sometimes as a part of the pattern. But always keep the reader more aware of what you are saying than of a constant, stultifying beat. Vary too much and the work has no shape. Vary not at all, and the meter and rhyme take over and meaning is lost.

When I sit up on a chair
I feel quite grand.
My head is higher in the air
Than when I stand.
The problem then for me is feet:
They and the floor just will not meet.

If you analyze the above, you will see that not all of the lines have the same number of feet and not all of the feet follow the same pattern. There is rhythm and there is rhyme, but the whole doesn't get so totally rhythmic that the sense of the words is lost.

When you write poetry and verse, have fun with rhyme, with meter, with ideas, ideas that will catch a child's fancy, that will exemplify aspects of a child's life and that will tell stories that are made more attractive and memorable by rhythmic patterns of language. Remember that subject matter and form must complement and reinforce each other. Rhyme and meter simply for the sake of rhyme and meter are absurd. But rhyme and meter that help to make an idea live, rhyme and meter that seem to exemplify what they say in a way that no prose statement could, have a place in literature for children.

STEP FOUR—EXPLORE MORE MODERN FORMS OF VERSE AND POETRY

As mentioned earlier, all poetry and verse has meter, but not all of it rhymes, and not all of it has a regular meter. In some poetry, especially much of that written in recent years, the meter is irregular, yet there is a sense of rhythm that underlies what is done.

What makes such poetry different from prose? It looks different, of course. It appears in short lines, like more rigidly patterned verse and poetry. But the main thing that separates such poetry from prose is the content. A poem presents a big way of looking at the world through a small event or idea expressed in a very few carefully planned words. A poem is a way of saying something important in a highly condensed and memorable form.

A poem can take an ordinary idea, an ordinary event, and make it a jumping-off place to an understanding of how that event fits into a total life or the world as a whole. Or it can take a singular event and show how one momentous occasion can help one leap from being one kind of person to another. And whatever it does, it does its work and makes its point clear without having to point out what it is doing. It may even demand that the reader give it more than one reading to make its full import clear. How well a child understands a given poem may depend on that child's maturity level. A poem that works well for a four-year-old may not be quite right yet for a three-year-old. But for the child who can grasp what is being said, the poem can be an avenue to a new understanding of the world, or at least of events in his or her own life.

I lost my mitten
in the store
and no one found it.
Now, I have one cold hand
And one big wonder —
Where do lost things go?
Who cares for them?
Who loves them now?

Poetry raises questions that it may or may not answer — the answer may have to reside in the child who reads or hears the poem. The above can have different implications for different children, depending on the child's own background. Verse, generally, may have only one interpretation, but a true poem can have many. A poem opens doors to thought through experiences that a child may have had or known about, and it invites children to think about implications of the experience that rest beyond the experience itself.

As mentioned, poems can be rhymed or unrhymed, strictly metered or unmetered — but do not let the relative freedom of what you are doing deceive you into thinking that any group of words put together in short lines is a poem. It is not. A poem, whether rhymed or unrhymed, metered or not, must open out, must suggest more than it says. You must think of the content of your poem as a metaphor for something larger. You must also set up a certain tension in the lines — you must constrict what you do in such a way that the whole almost seems to explode out of itself. When you have an image in your mind that you think will make a poem, ponder that image until you see just the core of it, then think of all the devices of poetry — the kinds of feet, the patterns of lines, the use of words as symbols — and arrive at the simplest, most direct way of saying what you want to say in a way that the devices of poetry most readily reinforce. The poem is a bud; it opens into a flower in the mind of the reader.

Experiment with ways of putting ideas into a concise, tense form where rhythm helps but does not constrict your expression. Write just a line or two at first — around an idea. Look about you for ideas, think about things that happen to children that have wider implications and try putting these into a brief, rhythmic setting. Write and revise and write again. Then think about what you really want to write. Are you ready to do it?

STEP FIVE—DECIDING WHAT AND HOW MUCH YOU WANT TO WRITE

You have one idea that haunts you. You are sure that it will make a poem. In fact, you have begun to work at it and you know that in the end you will be able to say what you want to say. But what are you going to do with one poem?

Before you decide you are going to be a children's poet, you must consider just what you are going to write. Are you going to tell a story in verse? All right, maybe, if it is well done. Are you going to create a long poem about something important to you, something that symbolizes life and its infinite possibilities— maybe a long poem about the wind? Will it offer good picture possibilities? Will it be written in a manner that will hold the reader's interest, not become boring because it uses the same pattern of lines and rhyme too consistently? All right, maybe, if it is well done. Or do you, perhaps, want to compose a group of individual poems that will together make a book? All right, too, if the poems will all be more or less at the same level so that a child at that level can enjoy them all.

Remember that a picture book generally has about 28 pages for text. If you are writing one long poem, it must break down into 28 pages or into 13 or 14 double-page spreads. If you are writing a group of poems, you will probably need to write at least 14 poems to fill those pages, though, if you like, you might write as many as 20 or even 25. The publisher will probably want at least one poem per spread, though a long poem might be broken up to cover two or even three spreads. Given the fact that most poems for children are short, however, it is best to prepare at least fourteen. If what you are choosing to write will not fill those 28 pages, you will not have a picture book text. This does not mean you can't write your poem, but you will want to submit it to a children's magazine rather than a children's book publisher. (If you do this, sell first serial rights only; keep book rights for yourself, because eventually you may write enough poems to make a book, and you may want to include this poem with the others.)

STEP SIX – BEGINNING TO WRITE YOUR POEM OR VERSE

How do you get started writing a poem? How do you get the essence of an idea down on paper in a way that will say something to someone else? First of all, you need to decide just what form to use. Rhyme and meter? Meter only? Free verse? How do you decide?

Some people begin a poem with an idea – one that comes from an event they have witnessed, an overheard statement, an idea that brings together two concepts in ways that seem new and interesting. If this is the way you begin, then get to the core of the idea. How would a child look at that idea? What would be important to a child? And at the same time, how does that idea relate to a more mature understanding of the world? Can that idea form a basis for a growing understanding of life? Or if this is to be a verse, what makes the idea interesting; how does the idea fit into a child's everyday experience?

Then think about the very least you need to say to get your idea across to someone else. How can rhythm help you? Will a bouncy rhythm help to make your meaning clear? Or will you need a more somber rhythm? What is the first thing that a reader must know to understand the rest of your verse or poem? What is the basis for what you are writing? This is what must come first. Then, almost as in nonfiction (poetry is considered nonfiction), you develop your idea, and at the end you finish with a statement that puts the whole into perspective. Make a list of basic ideas that must go into your poem, then establish the order in which they must come. Think of words and phrases that will give color and action and evocations of atmosphere in order to express some of what you want to say. What sort of pattern do these seem to require? What pattern will give the necessary explosive tension to the whole? What figures of speech will help you create the pictures you need to make your meaning clear? Gradually work your ideas into a pattern that seems to do what you want.

Other people begin to write a poem not only with an idea but with a line that comes to mind from somewhere – overheard, read, out of the blue. Sometimes all that is there is a tantalizing line that seems to demand to be part of a poem. If this is the case, think first about what that line means, where you think it ought to go. Is it the first line or the last line of the poem or verse — or is it a line repeated many times? What pattern does it call for? Think about that line a lot — in bed when you can't sleep, in line at the grocery store or the bank, waiting for a friend to arrive — until you know what it means to you and what ought to go with it. Then pattern your poem as if you had begun with an idea.

Whatever way you develop your poem, make the language you use in your writing colorful, evocative and fresh. Furthermore the words you use must express more than the meanings commonly given them. And the patterns you choose for those words must do more for your idea than carry out rhythm and maybe rhyme. If you are writing about a butterfly, for example, you will want short lines and a sprightly foot — to give the feeling of a fluttery butterfly. But if you are writing about an elephant, you may need a longer line and a more plodding foot. A poem about a hippo should probably look heavy and solid: long lines and maybe not too many of them in short squat verses. A poem about a giraffe might be tall and impressive, short lines and many of them, with no breaks between for separate verses. And the words used should match the form. The ideas you express must come upon the reader as a new image, a new way of looking at what may be — even to a child — an old idea. And yet, at the same time, it must seem simple and natural, as if the idea had existed in that form since the beginning of time.

It helps to express ideas in poetry and verse in ways that balance, in sentences and clauses that reflect each other in thought and in meter. Parallel ideas expressed in sentences with an interesting sense of balance can excite the reader's imagination as no flat statement can. Compare these two sets of lines:

> The kite swept, fleet, to sky
> Rose like a hawk at play.

Or:

> The kite once in the air
> Flew high without a care.

The first gives a more complete picture than the second; it is more memorable and more picturesque, though more difficult. The first may be on the way to being a part of a poem; the second is poor verse.

Of course, parallel statements will not always work; not every poem or verse can be written this way. But the basic premise remains: poetry and verse is more than rhyme and meter—it is a condensed form of speech that creates images in the mind of the reader, that uses words in ways that stir the imagination. It is a codification of feeling and sensitivity that will reinforce what others have thought and not expressed, or have never quite seen in just that way before. As such, for children it needs to be short, pithy, and yet graceful and open to a variety of interpretations. When writing a poem or a verse, you must use all the skills you have learned about writing, and add to this your own personal perceptions of what life is all about.

STEP SEVEN — REVISION

Even as you write, ideas for revision will begin to crop up. You may find yourself pondering each line, working to make the feet and line lengths come out right, trying to find the right rhyme, if your poem or verse does rhyme. And as you work, you will revise in order to fulfill the patterns you have set for yourself. Word will be substituted for word, phrase for phrase, and sentence for sentence. Some words will come out and no words will be put in their place because no new words are needed. A shorter, more rhythmic or more poetic sounding way of stating a given idea will occur, but that may necessitate changing something else, to make the meter or the parallelism or the rhyme work.

Because a poem is short, generally, and because so much revision is likely, you may prefer, even in these days of computers, to use pencil and paper. Pencil and paper will allow you to keep track of all of the various changes and versions that occur in the process of making the poem work. Sometimes you will find it very useful to have past versions available because a word or phrase that did not work in an earlier version may suddenly become the very thing that does work in a later version. And once in a while, after much revision, you may find yourself going back to the first version and starting all over.

Through all of this work, writing and revision, you must keep the vision in mind of the idea or the phrase that started the poem in the first place. The metaphor or simile that forms the basis for the poem, probably, should remain clear and uncorrupted in your mind, no matter how many times you revise, until a final version of the work matches the initial idea. Only when you believe you have put the initial inspiration into the best form possible, in the simplest and yet most telling manner, can you call your work done.

This is the initial revision. It is the revision that takes place simultaneously with the initial writing. It will be a rare occasion when you can sit down and simply write a poem or even a simple verse without making changes, substituting words, trying out different ways of saying the same thing, striving to find exactly the right words to capture what must be said. Accept this as part of writing a poem and enjoy the opportunity it presents to see how skillful you are in finding the words you need.

STEP EIGHT—LET THE WORK COOL

The poem may seem done. But is it? Does it say exactly what you wanted to say? Will it say what you wanted to say to someone else? To be sure that the poem is done, put it away for a time—a week, a month, even more—and then come back to it. How does it sound now? Does it still reverberate in your mind with the strength of your initial vision? Does it seem natural, unforced and yet rhythmic and full of meaning? Do all the words seem right? Does the basic structure of the poem reinforce the meaning—or is the structure simply superimposed on the idea? In other words, if you are speaking of a skyscraper, does the poem look squat and rotund instead of tall and stately? Are the words you have used rounded and squashy rather than elevated and slim? Think about it. What do the words of your poem, the ones you have chosen and the way you have put them together, say, in addition to their meaning? Are there too many words? Too few? How does the poem speak to you now? Is it really finished?

If the poem holds up for you, let someone whose judgment you trust read it. Don't stand over the person, or sit in the same room while the poem is being read, trying to judge the person's reaction from the look on his or her face. Give it to the reader, let the person read it at leisure, and comment at leisure, when he or she has had time to reflect on what has been read. Don't argue with the reader. Remember that a poem should be capable of various interpretations; each reader has a right to whatever opinion the poem engenders. Instead, reflect on that opinion, good or bad, trying to discern what led to whatever was said. And then reflect on whether or not your poem or verse did what you intended. If yes—do with it whatever you intended to do. If not, you may want to revise again.

You may even want to have your poem read to a child at this time, though that is not as valid an exercise as you might think. Remember, this poem is destined for a picture book of some sort, and it does not yet have the pictures that will help hold the child's attention, help interpret the poem, and help stir the child's imagination. Also, children differ in their tastes. What one child likes, another does not. A skilled adult reader can be a better judge of what you have done than a child, even though the poem is destined for children.

STEP NINE—DECIDING WHAT TO DO WITH YOUR POEM

Did you think before you began your poem about what you wanted it to be? Have you written a number of poems that one way or another you think might be put together into a book? Or have you written a long story poem or verse that you hope will, in itself, make a book?

If you have only one short poem, you should probably try to submit it to a magazine like *Ladybug* or *Cricket* that publishes children's verse. But if you have one long poem that you think might make a book, ask yourself these questions: Will this break up well into pages? Is it long enough to be a complete book? Are there a variety of picture possibilities? Is the subject strong enough to carry a complete book? Will what you have written make sense to children—and to their parents—even if it is nonsense verse? (Not a bad idea, remember that children like humor and they like what is clearly nonsense to them—but make sure they will recognize it as nonsense.) Does what you have written bear re-reading? Can you see it as a book? If you can answer yes to all of these questions, you may be ready for a publisher.

If you have written a group of poems or verses, you must ask yourself some of the same questions as you would if you had written one long work, but you must ask some others as well: Are all of your poems for children of the same age and experience level? Do the poems or verses relate to each other in some way—nature poems, holiday poems, family and growing up poems, school and play poems, friend poems, or poems that reflect the outlook on life of one given child? There needs to be some "handle" that will allow prospective buyers to understand what they are getting. This does not mean that the poems must all directly concern themselves with the same subject in a given book, but it certainly helps publisher, bookseller and buyer if there is some sort of tag that the book can be given that will help identify the contents. Again, you must ask yourself if the poems lend themselves to variety of illustration and to re-reading—with, perhaps, growing awareness in the reader of the depths of meaning that you have introduced into each poem. Can you imagine these poems together in a book? Would you buy such a book for your children or the children of friends or relatives if the poems were written by someone else? (Even if the book costs $14.95?)

STEP TEN—FINAL REWRITE—READY FOR AN EDITOR

Your verses or your poems—or single verse or poem if such is the case—meet all the criteria. You are convinced that what you have is ready to be a book. Then it is time to prepare your manuscript for submission.

Read your work again. Put it away for a day or two and read it yet again. Make any changes that seem absolutely necessary. But if what you have done has seemed good to you and to others, don't be too quick to make last-minute changes. Sometimes they are a mistake, born of nervousness as one thinks about a total stranger reading one's work.

Type up or print out your manuscript, double- or triple-spaced. If it is one long poem or verse, type it just as you would a story, with no breaks for book pages, other than the normal verse breaks that the work contains (if it does contain them). If you have a group of verses or poems, type them one to a page, and put them in the order you think they should be read. Number the pages, as you would the pages of any other manuscript. Give the work a title. Your finished manuscript should look like a manuscript for any other form of writing—page number and name on each page, etc.

Do not include picture suggestions unless something in a text demands a picture to make the meaning clear. If so, make your picture description factual and as short as possible.

Where do you send it? To a publisher that publishes poetry, of course. More about that in the chapter on selling your picture book manuscript. Read it, do what is needed, then get out two envelopes — one for sending the material and one for return — package your work and take it to the post office. Good luck.

SKILL SEVEN

Writing Essays and Concept Books

W hat is an essay or a concept picture book? How can children enjoy something that sounds so sophisticated? Well, such a book is not as adult as it sounds, and can be among the most popular books a child encounters. Such books are books for young children that deal with moral and ethical principles, attitudes about conduct, and appreciation of the world in which the child exists.

There are many kinds: books about going to bed at night, about encounters with baby-sitters, about dealing with fears of all kinds, about the joy of discovery, about growing up and doing new things, about learning new things, about relationships with parents and siblings, about almost anything that a child might wonder or worry about. Such books can expound the delights of wandering in the woods on a snowy night, the joy of finding out that the dark is friendly and not fierce, the helpful knowledge that sorrow as well as joy is a part of life. They present aspects of love, trust, adventure, and social attitudes toward others that are important to children. And they also explore and help to develop aspects of humor and nonsense that can make a child's life infinitely more pleasurable.

There are many subjects that puzzle children or aspects of personality they need to develop that cannot be touched by ordinary nonfiction because the factual basis for them is elusive; that poetry cannot always effectively explore because they demand a more explicit approach than poetry allows; and that fiction can undertake only in stories that can easily become too didactic (though concept books, too, should avoid being obviously didactic — see Step Three). These are the subjects that essays and concept books present, and they do so in an interesting and childlike manner, one that gives children both enjoyment and ideas to ponder.

If this area of children's picture books puzzles you, if you can't recall seeing any that seem to fall into this category, go to your library or bookstore and look for some. Among the more recent titles you may find are: *Everything Has a Place* by Patricia Lillie; *The Moon Was the Best* by Charlotte Zolotow; *Good Days, Bad Days* by Catherine Anholt; *Mama, Do You Love Me?* by Barbara M. Joosse; *Samuel Todd's Book of Great Inventions* by E.L. Konigsburg; and *Cowboy Dreams* by Dayal Kaur Khalsa. Your nearest children's librarian or children's bookseller can undoubtedly suggest other titles that fit into this important category.

If you decide to write such a book it is probably because you have already seen the need for children to come to understand a given idea and have rejected other ways of presenting it. For every writer of picture book texts there is always the possibility that someday an idea will demand this format. Everyone who wants to do such a book should realize that there is a place for it, and it can be done in ways that appeal to children. Here are some steps that may help in creating one.

STEP ONE—DECIDE IF THE BOOK IS NEEDED

You have an idea that doesn't seem to work in any form that you have tried. You want to assure a child that no matter what happens, his mother and father will love him. (Not always true in today's society, but true enough that for most children it is a valid reassurance.) The story you tried was sickly sweet; you couldn't stand it. Nonfiction offered you no way in. And you wanted something more direct than poetry. So what you need to write is a concept book. Is it a valid idea? you ask. Yes, you decide.

Why did you come to that decision? For most kinds of children's books, it is not wholly necessary to know today's children. It is enough to find the child within you. But a concept book often does demand some understanding of childhood today. There are uncertainties and yearnings and confusions that belong to the childhoods of every time and place, but most of them were expressed and felt in somewhat different ways in other times. To write a concept book for today, one must anchor it in today's milieu. So today we write about love in terms of divorce, stepparents, and day-to-day not year-to-year experience. We appreciate nature in small blocks and not in large sweeps of landscape. We think of the dark of night in many contexts: at home, on city streets, in country meadows. And all are different.

When you decide you want to write a concept book, you must not only choose a topic that is important to you, but one that means something to a child of today in the world in which he or she lives. From where do such ideas come? Has your life been touched by a child's problem? Have you seen children that you long to set upon a straight path? Do you decry the lack of plain, simple fun in many children's lives? Have you read enough about certain problems of childhood in newspaper accounts that you yearn to bring your own thoughts to the matter? Do you believe that the message you want to convey will give a child hope and confidence and security rather than fear and timidity? Have you tried to incorporate your ideas into another kind of book and failed? If so, maybe you do need to write a concept book.

STEP TWO – NARROWING YOUR SUBJECT

Like every other kind of picture book, your concept book will be short. You can't cover all of even a relatively small idea in one book. Consequently, you must get quickly to the core of what you want to say. How to do this? Think first of your subject as a whole. Maybe your subject is *love*. Think of the areas of that subject that most touch children's lives: family — mother, father, siblings, other relatives — and friends. You might be able to present all of this by showing how each contributes to the child's well-being. Or you might want to narrow your view a little more — to just mother and father, perhaps. But think beyond this. What is it you want to say about love? Do you want to define it? Or do you want to discuss what love does for people, love in general? Do you want to discuss varieties of love? What aspect of love will you choose to present? You can't do it all. And the more you think about love, the more you will find that there is much to explore. How do you decide what to do?

Your decision must be based on why you want to write this book, and why you think children will want to encounter what you have to say. What do you think children need to know? Do they need to know first and foremost that they are surrounded by love at all times — or do you think that there are enough children not so surrounded that you would prefer to come to your subject another way? Do children need to understand, first and foremost, that they are entitled to love and that they must seek a place where they can find it? Or you might decide that what children need to understand is that love begets love, and that acts of love on the part of a child can bring love in return. Or do you just want to explore the kinds of love a child may encounter? Think through your subject. You may want to list all of the possible approaches your book might take. Then explore your own thinking to see which of those approaches will be the best vehicle for your message.

No matter what it is you want to write about, you need to investigate the ways it might be presented and discover the one best for you. You may want to write about how to laugh at what is really funny and not laugh at what seems odd but is not actually funny. Or you may want to explain that sleep is necessary to every living creature (or at least to most living creatures — I'm not sure that an amoeba sleeps and I gather a shark probably does not). Whatever your subject, you must explore it for its potential, then center down to the core of what you want to say.

STEP THREE — AVOIDING COMMON PROBLEMS

You have a message you want to convey. The temptation is to blurt it out in a simple, direct manner so that the child who encounters your book will be sure to get the point. Don't! Sermons have their place, but not in books for children. Children get enough of them from other sources. Books should provide children with an opportunity to grow, but most growing takes place subtly. Too forceful an approach can breed defiance.

How do you get your message across? You won't have a story to cover up what you want to say. How can a concept book carry your ideas without preaching? There are a number of ways. Most of them involve some of the same figures of speech that make poetry come alive and speak to children.

Humor is one way. Exaggeration and silliness often can make a point far more effectively than a serious lecture. For the child who is afraid of the dark, for example, a book that documents ways of avoiding thinking about the dark or a game of imagining all the silly things that might be hiding in the dark can be better than an attempt to prove that there is no danger in the dark and a lecture about facing one's fears. Does your subject lend itself to humor? Can you think of a funny way to present your ideas, one that will get your audience laughing?

Creating a mood of beauty and delight is a second way to get around being preachy. For that same child, the one who is afraid of the dark, a mood piece can dwell lovingly on beautiful things that can be experienced only in the dark. Mood pieces use alliteration and simile and metaphor to create their moods. They draw word pictures that make the events or objects they describe seem real and wonderful. In writing such a piece, every word must be selected with care not only to give the exact meaning desired, but also to carry with it the exact connotation needed to reinforce that meaning and to blend with the other words and phrases to create the rhythm and sound that amplifies the basic intent of the work. Like poetry, this sort of concept book uses language in that special way that makes pattern and rhythm a part of the meaning of the whole.

A third way of getting around being preachy is to be non-committally factual. In other words — going back to the child who is afraid of the dark — a short book that explores the reasons for the dark and things the child can look for that make the difference between light and dark (almost a science book) can make the right child more interested in the phenomenon of dark than in the fear of the dark. Such a book could also explore all the dark places a child might enjoy thinking about and never considered as being dark — outer space, a closet full of toys when the door is closed, the place under the ground where seeds are put and from which they grow, the underground nest where mice live, the other side of the world when we are in the light. These might be presented one to a page or one to a spread, with enough text to explain each and a lead in to the next item.

When your mother put those tulip bulbs into the ground last fall, they stayed there in the dark all the long winter. But when spring came, even in the dark they felt that warm days had come again. And they began to grow. Soon they came out into the light, just the way you get up out of bed in the morning. And after a while they had flowers. But tulip bulbs were not the only live things that spent the winter in the dark under the ground. / [End of page] / In the bottom of little ponds everywhere, frogs were spending the winter in the dark, too. Etc. Etc. Etc.

Such a book might end with a child being put to bed in the dark, glad to have this happen because things grow in the dark. Not preachy, just factual. The trick is in assembling the various kinds of events and places that will appeal to children and make them want to be a part of what is happening.

Other kinds of concept books—books that make children love the out-of-doors, enjoy working with other children, look forward to family get-togethers, or accept visits to the dentist—can be handled in some of these same ways, or they can be approached in ways that the subjects themselves suggest.

Being preachy may be the greatest trap the concept book writer can blunder into, but it is not the only problem that can arise. There are those who try to be too cute. (*Those teeny-weeny stars up there in the sky are not afraid to be out at night in the dark.*) There are those who strain too much to make a presentation different. (*Draw a star on a piece of paper. Cut it out. Take it to the window. It's just like the stars up in the sky, isn't it? But this star is yours. It's going to watch over you all night long.*) Nonsense. That is straining in a way that every child will reject.

Your concept book needs to be as simple and natural and smooth as well-sanded wood. Different is good if it comes naturally. The essence of a good concept book is ease and simplicity of approach.

STEP FOUR—ORGANIZING YOUR TEXT— PATTERN AND PRESENTATION

You know what you want to write. You have thought about your overall theme; you have centered that theme down to a core focus; and you have even thought about the way in which your premise can be presented. You are almost ready to write your book. But not quite! You still need to decide on specifics for your book, and you need to put them into an overall pattern. Even though you are not quite ready to write, you may want to get out pencil and paper at this point. It is time to make some notes to yourself, out of which the final manuscript may come.

Sit down and think about your book—or take a walk and think about your book—do whatever stimulates you and allows your thoughts to emerge. Brainstorm, write down, or store in your memory if that is better for you, all of the items you can think of that might be a part of your book. You may want to do this over a period of days or even weeks. Every time a new idea comes to you, note it, or store it in your memory. Don't fall in love with any ideas, not yet. Think of them all as having equal value, even if you know deep inside that some are not as good as others.

Think of this gathering of ideas as popping popcorn. The kernels pop slowly at first, then gather speed and begin to pop at a great rate, and finally they slow down, as most of the kernels that are going to pop have done so. When the popping begins to slow, it is time to stop the process and eat the popped corn. You may find that ideas come slowly at first. But once you have started thinking in all directions, ideas will come much faster—more ideas than you thought possible. Then finally, ideas will approach more slowly, and many of them will seem to be duplicates of ones you have already noted. Then you are ready to pattern your product and decide what ought to go into the manuscript itself.

Read through the ideas you have noted for yourself, or review them in your mind—though if that's where they are, you might want to write them down at this point so you have them in front of you. Think about the core of the idea you want to present. Maybe you want to explore parallels between city living and country living as a child might see them. Your plan is to have one facing page with the city and the other with the country. You find you have amassed at least fifty such comparisons. Which of your ideas best exemplify the basic similarities and differences a child might want to explore? Cat in the house versus cat in the barn? Maybe. Quiet road in front of the house versus street with heavy traffic? Maybe. Mother and father who work at home versus parents who go to work? Maybe. Woods on the farm versus woods in the park? Maybe. The dangers of being kidnapped in the city versus the danger of getting caught in the farm machinery on the farm? Probably not, not just because they are negative but because they would be hard for the child who did not live in the city or who did not live in the country to understand—they might have too much impact.

Explore your ideas. Ask yourself which can be presented in the most concrete manner, which lend themselves to the best picture variety. Of the above: cats, certainly; road versus street, only maybe because the concept might not be child-related enough — though it could be if the city child said *I have to cross my street at the corner, where there's a light* and the country child said *Sometimes I have to wait to cross the road in front of my house until the cows have all come home to the barn.* The trick is to keep the text child-centered, to keep the examples of whatever you are doing concrete, and to involve as much action and activity as possible.

When you can, use metaphor, simile and other figures of speech. These will help make your ideas concrete. Going back to the city/country example, if you were to contrast city and country woods you might say: (City) *Sometimes I walk through the park with my mother. There are tall trees all around full of birds.* (Country) *Almost every day in summer I go to play in our woods. There are hiding places among the trees that are like little houses for me.*

Strive for variety of content — one woods scene is enough, one barn scene is enough, one street scene may be enough, etc. — and for examples that will take about the same number of words and sentences to present, with about the same vocabulary level. That city versus country danger sequence might not work, for example, for this reason, too — it might require too much explanation and a different kind of vocabulary than the other examples. Furthermore, it would offer a different atmosphere and mood than most of the other ideas that might occur to you. Concept books depend for much of their effect on mood and atmosphere. So the ideas must blend in this way as well as in others.

To sum up, when you plan what your manuscript will contain, the whole should be a unit; it should all focus on your main theme, but at the same time offer variety enough to keep the reader interested and give him or her a panoply of perspectives, all within a frame of mood and atmosphere that help the reader understand how you feel about what you are saying. Most of all, the way you present your thoughts should fit the world in which the prospective reader lives. You should give your reader an experience that will fit her or his level of life. You are not going to talk about city tax rates versus country tax rates. Taxes may affect children, but not in ways that one can portray in a picture book. So think about the children you know and the child you were and ask, will the elements you have chosen really express your thoughts to a child?

You may find — if you have done a good job of brainstorming —

that you have more material than you need, even when you have applied all of the above criteria. Good! Better too much than too little! Writing out of abundance is easier than having to stretch to fill your pages. So, if you have too much, be glad, and then begin to cut further.

Experiment — in your mind or even roughly on paper — with the various potential parts of your book to see which actually do work together in the smoothest, most logical fashion. If you were writing the city/country book, would you keep it to a child's actual activities — playing with cats, visiting the woods, enjoying friends, going shopping, watching rain, etc. — or would you also include material about parents working at home and parents working away — with maybe child care of some sort for the city child? If this is to be a quiet mood piece, maybe the daily activities are best; but if this is to be a book about the sharp differences between city and country living, parental employment and other information of that nature belong.

When you have chosen the examples that best suit the book you want to write, it is time to decide in what order they should appear. If the city/country book looks at daily activities, do you begin with getting up in the morning and end with going to bed at night? Or if it takes a wider look at the contrasts, do you begin with what one sees out one's window in the morning and then move to house versus apartment building, parents at home and away, friends at day care and friends on the next farm, etc.? In any case, the simplest and easiest — getting up in the morning, looking out the window — is where to begin. Then you move to the more far-flung, going from the ideas that are nearest to every child's experience to those that may demand a bit of stretching.

The city/country book does not demand many transitions. Each spread can exist on its own with the overall theme drawing it all together. But other kinds of concept books demand a bridge between one example and the next or may even need to show that one idea builds on another. If you were to do a mood book about the city and the country in the sort of format where held one way the book explores one idea and turned over and held the other way, explores another (each ending, of course, in the middle — where the two parts meet), you might need to build from one idea to the next:

The country is where all the food you eat is grown. Farmers live in the country. They plant seeds in the ground, which grow and make corn and beans and spinach. They raise chickens and cows, etc. / The city is where the clothes you wear and the toys you play with and the books you read are made. People make them in big buildings called factories. These people live in great big buildings, too, etc.

See which of your examples work together best, which allow for the easiest transitions from one idea to the next, which seem to enlarge your idea from one segment to the next. Try putting your ideas together in a number of different ways until you find the way that will make it easiest for you to write your book. That is the way you should choose.

STEP FIVE—THINK ABOUT PICTURES

You are now almost ready to write a very good first draft of your book. But first you need to take one more look at the components you have chosen. You need to look at them and think about pictures. You have probably already thought about this to some extent. You know that someone must create a series of pictures to illustrate your text, and those pictures must be interesting to children and offer variety from page to page and spread to spread. But now you should give concentrated thought to this need.

Look at the elements you have chosen to make up your text and ask yourself if they lend themselves to illustration—and to varied illustrations. Will an artist be able to create not only decorative illustrations, but illustrations that may extend your text? If your text is to be entirely abstract, with nothing at all concrete, an illustrator is going to have a hard time finding pictures to draw, and children may have a hard time understanding what you say. If you discover that your text may be too abstract to allow for relevant illustration, think about making your text more concrete. Can you present the same elements in a more concrete manner— in terms of people or animals or objects of some sort? You need not turn your concept book into a story, but you can use concrete examples as metaphors or similes. How you do this will depend on what subject you have chosen. A book on love would need to describe love in terms of various relationships between people (or between animals disguised as people). A book on the dark and its wonders would need to make those wonders apparent with concrete items and events—stars and shadows and the new shapes things acquire in the dark.

Think about pictures. Know they are possible. But don't make up your mind as to exactly what they must be unless something is necessarily omitted in your text and the information must come in a picture. Just make sure your text is sharp and clear enough that an illustrator will interpret what you have done in the way you mean for it to be interpreted. Make sure your adjectives and adverbs, your nouns and verbs are precise, your sentences are unambiguous, and your rhythms create the right mood, and an illustrator will know what you want.

STEP SIX—WRITING THE FIRST DRAFT

By this time you should be very familiar with what you want to do. You should be ready to get it down on paper. Get comfortable. Organize your tools. And begin.

You have already established a pattern, a sort of outline for your text. But now you must determine what approach you will take to your work. The actual writing itself should have a pattern, just as the elements of the text fall into a pattern. The writing pattern you choose will give the piece a sense of unity and will determine the mood of the finished piece. There are a number of ways to do this. Here are a few:

A Parallel Presentation

If you are offering a series of ideas around a central theme that are roughly equal and do not demand a specific sequence (or even if they do, but would benefit from repetition), then you might find that you can approach each separate item in much the same way until you get to the end, when you may want to come to a conclusion that seals in the rest by being written in a different way. *(I love my mother because. . . . And she loves me just because I'm me; I love my father because. . . . And he loves me just because I'm me; I love my grandma because. . . . And she loves me just because I'm me*; etc., until the end—*I love my cat just because she is my cat. And she loves me because I hug her and let her sit on my bed.)* In doing this, however, you must be careful to get enough variety into the text to keep it from being too predictable. Don't strain for variety, but work hard at creating a variety that seems natural in the elements themselves. The pattern of presentation will not grow dull if the content is sometimes surprising: the reasons the child loves mother, father, grandma, etc., rather than the fashion in which the words are placed on the page. Think about what a child would think, what a child would say. Use this as a basis for what you do.

A Sequenced Presentation

Some ideas demand that they be presented in sequence, each part building on what went before until the end is reached. When this is the case, begin at the beginning, which is where the child reader is before he has encountered your book. You take a first step, then a second, then a third and so on, each step moving a bit more into the core of your idea. In a sequenced presentation, you will not couch each part in the same pattern of words. Instead, you will lure your readers on by couching each segment in words and phrases that convey a sense of action and excitement, that reflect your own enthusiasm for what is being presented. And you will connect the segments, one thought to the next, in interesting ways. *(Come with me to the woods. / I see a squirrel, do you? / Let's run down the path where the squirrel went. Oh! Look at the baby squirrel! / And look there—there's a baby tree. Did you know that big trees were babies once? / And here are some babies that never grow up. Moss that grows on stones always stays small*, etc., until the end—in a book designed to introduce wonders of the woods to a child—*Time to go home, but we can come to the woods again. You never know what you'll see in the woods. Every woods is different from every other woods. Going to the woods is always an adventure.)* This is only one example of the kind of thing that can be presented in a sequential way. Many kinds of ideas must be built one thought upon another. The trick is to make each step of the way so attractive through the action suggested, the visions painted, that the reader is lured on. Remember it is language, the pace and rhythm of sentences, that does this, as well as the sentence content. Make your text move from page to page.

A Surprise Presentation

Sometimes a book can make its point most effectively by making the ending of each segment of the book a surprise. Generally such a book is set up with a question or a mystery of some sort on a right-hand page and the solution on the following left-hand page, where it cannot be seen until the page is turned. Or a double-page spread can set the mystery, and the next double spread solve it. The problem must be stated succinctly and dramatically, challenging the reader; it must be a question that will intrigue a child. Give the question a twist that makes it appealing. If possible make it seem as if it is coming from the reader, so the reader is involved (see below). The language of this sort of book can vary, depending on the subject: it can be humorous; it can be mock serious or exaggerated; it can be truly serious; but it should be consistent throughout the book. There will probably be an element of the parallel in your text if you write this kind of book; but there will be elements of the sequential as well, building to the final question and the final climax. Whatever manner you choose to present your material, it should be on a child's level, and the answers should be based on a child's ability to understand. (*What is that awful shape? [child in bed in the dark] Is it an elephant? / Yes, it's an elephant. It's an elephant-sized toy chest./ What is that thing that moves by the window? Is it a monster? / No, it's only part of a monster. It's a branch of that monster tree outside the window./ What's that fuzzy thing in the corner? Is it a big, big bird? / No, it's only the nest of a bird. It's the chair a bird like you sits on in the daytime* and so on until some climactic question and answer proves once and for all that the dark holds only pleasant secrets.) Surprise presentations can be fun for children, but you should make almost a game of what is going on in the book so that there is real delight in the discoveries that live on the other side of the page.

A Mood Presentation

Some ideas demand that the text create a mood that infuses the whole and lets the child's experience be one of emotion as well as thoughtful understanding. These might include the joys of the dark (different from the surprise presentation, of course), the wonders of friendship, the specialness of sharing, etc. A mood presentation can be sequential, but it almost never has a parallel construction or a surprise element. Rather, if this type of presentation is your choice, try to use language in such a way that the reader will feel and experience what you feel and experience. Your object here should be to give a child an emotional experience that he might not otherwise come to, but that will be of help to him in understanding the world. Here, choice of words and patterns of sentences are the most important elements. Heavy words—*m* and *w* words, words that carry with them a sense of slowness and thoughtfulness—will create a mood of depth and concern—as will ponderous rhythms and longish sentences. Light words—*e* and *t* and *l* words, words that trip over the tongue swiftly—will create a sense of joy and gaity and the elements of happy days, as will short bouncing rhythms. Slippery words—*s* and *th* and *sw* words, words that swish forth—and sentences that slither along will convey the idea of sly movement or swift movement. It is a mistake to overuse alliteration, but there is nothing that works quite as well, when carefully done, to create mood in a sentence, in a paragraph, in a work as a whole.

The important thing in a mood piece is to determine the mood wanted, to keep the approach to language at about the same level throughout, though it may vary in pace from place to place, and to build in a measured way to the climax of understanding that you want. Here, as in so many other kinds of writing for picture book age children, you begin where the child is and gradually bring that child into the experience you are creating. Write your first sentence in the mood and pattern you want to establish, and keep that first sentence in mind as you write all that follows. The whole should seem to be cut of the same cloth.

There are other ways a concept book can be organized. No rule says that a book must be organized in any one special way. The nature of the material should dictate the style of organization. The important thing is that the material *be* organized. Of equal importance is that the whole be as brief as possible and at the same time cover its material in such a way that the reader will understand what is being said and react as the author wishes. This involves making sure that every word and every sentence carries the meaning intended and that each sentence forwards the concept in some way. Before you write a sentence, know what it must say and what feelings it must also convey. Then consider the words that will do this best and the pattern of sentence that will best give your thoughts shape. Will a simple sentence do the job? Do you need modifiers for your subject or your verb? Will there be a phrase that needs a conjunction? If so, which conjunction will convey just exactly the right relationship between the main clause and the phrase? Or is this to be a compound sentence? If so what are its parts and what relationship does each bear to the other? What words in each part will complement words in the other part to balance the parts and give the reader more than the mere meaning of the words? Make each word, each phrase, each clause, each sentence bear as much meaning as possible. At the same time, guard against creating a piece in which the shades of meaning are so dense that the whole cannot be grasped at least on one level at a first reading. You are not writing a philosophic essay — you are writing a children's picture book.

STEP SEVEN — EVALUATING THE RESULTS

You have finally finished that first draft. You are sure it is the concept book text of the century. But is it? Read it through now. Even on the first reading, you may find things you want to change. Make those changes, but do not lose the original. You may eventually want to salvage some of what you did in the beginning.

When you read your essay, read it as if you had never seen it before. And think about it. Remember what it was you wanted to do in this book. Is the meaning clear? Do the words and sentences work together as a unit? Does the whole achieve its goal without preaching? Does each segment have picture possibilities? Are there places that could be better? Think about what you have done. Does a totally different way of achieving your goal suggest itself to you? If it does, try it. Do major changes in what you have done suggest themselves? If so, try them. But, do not lose that first draft. This was the way you initially conceived the book, and in the end it may turn out to have more validity than now seems likely. On the other hand, your new changes may prove to be what you really want to do. Change all you like, but keep all versions of what you are doing available.

Whether you try sweeping changes in your first draft, or you decide you like it just as is, chances are that your early readings of the manuscript, right after or soon after you finish it, will not give you as clear a picture of what you have done as a reading some days — or even some weeks — later. Put the manuscript away for as long as you can bear to do so. Then bring it out, reread it, trying to forget what you had in mind when you wrote it. What does it say to you? How valid does it sound? Then remember what you wanted to do. What changes seem necessary to reach that goal? If you made several versions at the time you wrote the piece, which now sounds best to you? Analyze words, sentences, paragraphs — but most of all try to abstract yourself from the work, to think of it as a work by someone else, to look at the manuscript as a whole, as a unit. What doesn't quite fit that whole? What words, sentences or paragraphs don't seem to fit the level of diction that most of the piece uses? What parts of the whole do not connect as well as they might to other parts of the whole? Where, in other words, are the holes and where are the parts that don't fit in with the other parts? Are there places where you indulged yourself and included something that really does not belong in the work at all?

From your perspective as a new reader, as a person in whom the glow of creation has passed and in whom a spirit of critical review can flourish, analyze what you have done. Choose the version that seems best and revise it to fit your new vision. Or you may want to do as some authors do: sit down and write the whole all over again, writing from a more intimate knowledge of the whole than you did the first time. What you do, and how you do it, is up to you and to what feels comfortable and necessary to you. The important thing is that you take this further look and revise in ways that seem necessary and important.

If you have the stomach for it, you might even put it away and come back to it in the same fashion once again. But don't revise endlessly. If you do, there will come a time when nothing will sound right because you know the whole too well; you can no longer see what is there. Revise when you finish, revise once after a time of rest, and maybe a second time after another time of rest, but do not revise, at least not without another point of view, beyond that time.

STEP EIGHT—CHECKING WITH OTHERS

Whom do you trust when it comes to manuscript evaluation? When you have taken your manuscript as far as you can go, when you think that maybe it is done, is the time to seek help. The help you seek should be knowledgeable adult help. Reading a manuscript to your grandchildren is no basis for deciding that nothing needs to be done. Your grandchildren would probably love the telephone book if you read it to them. And even having someone else read your manuscript to a child is no way to test it; in fact this can be unfair to you because what you have is not yet a book. A finished book has pictures to help to keep a child's attention on the material and help the child understand and appreciate what is being said. So it is a knowing adult that you need: another writer whose judgment you trust; perhaps a teacher of young children who has good literary judgment and an understanding of the fact that this is a text designed to be accompanied by pictures that are not there; perhaps a friend or relative who has been helpful in the past. Or you may be in a writing group or a writing class to which you can read what you have done. If you have such a person or group, now is the time to acquaint them with your manuscript.

If you choose to get the reactions of one or more other people, deal with their opinions judiciously. Do not necessarily accept all they have to say. Remember, you are the author, not they. But they can be helpful in answering some questions that you as the author cannot. No matter how hard you try to distance yourself from your work, you cannot do so completely. Therefore you need to ask: What does this manuscript mean to you? How does it make you feel? Did you understand the manuscript? Were there places that seemed vague and uncertain to you or not clear enough to be readily understood? Were there portions of the manuscript that seemed too long? Were there things that seemed not to belong at all? It is no help to have someone say they like the manuscript—or they don't like it. What you need to get from others is specific information about how the manuscript works, whether or not it achieves its goal.

When you have received whatever opinions you seek, make what changes you think are necessary in the manuscript to remedy the defects that your readers found.

STEP NINE—CHECKING WITH EXPERTS

Most concept books will not need expert consultation, but a few may. If you are dealing with death or failure or other difficult problems that face children, you may want to let a child psychologist or a teacher or someone else who knows how children react to difficult circumstances read what you have done and tell you whether or not your book might prove helpful. There may also be bits of information in your work that may best be checked by an expert in one field or another. It is unlikely that a concept picture book will have such detailed information on any one subject (after all, it is not a standard nonfiction book) that confirmation by an expert will be needed, but it is not an impossible situation. So, if you are in any way unsure of something you have said, try to have it checked by someone who will bring knowledge of that unsure area to the work and either confirm what you said or tell you where you went wrong. If you do this, you will, of course, want to make the changes suggested.

However—one caution—even an expert in a given field may want you to write the book in the way he or she would have done it and not in the way you have chosen to do it. But you are the author. Your way of writing is your way of writing. What you want from the expert is not information on how to write your book but information on very factual matters in or about your work, not on its organization, style or even choice of subject.

STEP TEN—DECIDING THE MANUSCRIPT IS FINISHED

By this time you are tired of your manuscript. Or at least you should be. It is time to call it done even if you want to revise it one more time. After revising at the behest of friends and literary advisors and experts (if it has been necessary)—do not revise further. If you still feel unsure of what you have done, write the whole thing again, trying to take care of what you think is wrong. Then put both versions away and come back to them in no less than a month, and decide which you prefer. Too much rewriting kills the vitality of a work. Do not revise your book into its grave. Revise, yes. Everyone needs to revise. But know when revision should end.

What you need to do now is retype—or reprint from your computer—the manuscript in its final form. There is no need for you to type what you see as separate pages on separate pieces of paper, nor is there any need for you to indicate what pictures you see (unless certain pictures are essential to understanding the manuscript). Simply type the whole, double-spaced on one side of the sheet—triple-spacing, perhaps, between paragraphs or between what you think of as separate pages. When you have a fair copy ready, check it for typos and for missing words. Make sure that it has a title page, that your name and a page number appear on each page. And then you are ready to think about sending the manuscript to an editor.

Marketing Your Picture Book Text

Your text is finished. You've written, revised, put the whole aside, revised some more, and now you believe that nothing more can be done — at least not at present. It is time for an editor to see it. It is time to try to sell your manuscript.

If you have sold a manuscript before, your decision as to where your manuscript should go may be an easy one. You may simply send it to your editor. But if you have not published before, or if you believe that for some reason you cannot send your current manuscript to a previous publisher, you must do your best to find a suitable place for your completed work, and you must do it in accordance with standard practices for submissions. Here are the steps you might take:

STEP ONE — SOME THINGS YOU MIGHT HAVE DONE IN ADVANCE

When you submit a manuscript, it is always helpful to be able to say that you have been published before. It is also a help to you in knowing how to reach an editor and what to expect when you have done so. It is not necessary for you to have been published by a national publisher to say that you have had experience. Many authors have had their first publication in local newspapers or in small local magazines. Some have written for children's magazines and story papers. Writing something and having it printed or published at your own expense does not qualify as real experience, but writing something (and maybe getting paid for it) for the children's page of a local newspaper or even the publication of some organization to which you belong does count. If your local newspaper does not have a children's page — not even weekly or monthly—find other authors interested in publishing for children and together suggest the idea of a page to the newspaper editor. Some editors may not like the idea, but others may find it a way to accustom a young audience to newspaper reading.

Your local library can tell you about other local publications that might value your contributions. You may own a copy, or you may find at your library a publication called *Children's Writer's & Illustrator's Market*; this book may help. The library may also have other directories of magazines and periodicals published in all parts of the nation. Some of these are divided by category. Check wherever you can for publications that accept material for children and write to any that sound interesting to find out what they are accepting. Don't necessarily concentrate on the large, well-known magazines for children. Look for some of the smaller magazines and periodicals, which may receive fewer submissions. If you find that some of those you approach take unsolicited manuscripts, send not picture book manuscripts but short stories to them. They may be glad to get what you send. You may get a little money in return. And you will have been published. You may also make contact with an editor who will help you develop your style and learn how to write for children.

Long before your manuscript is completed, you may also have joined a critique group. Many authors find such groups helpful— even Newbery Award winners. (The Newbery Award is given to the text of a book deemed by a panel of librarians to be the best contribution to children's literature published in a given year. It is the highest award for a children's book text given in the United States.) If you can find a group of five or six writers who are interested in children's books, you can help each other. You may locate such a group by consulting your local children's librarian or children's book store, or by joining the Society of Children's Book Writers and Illustrators, which tries to put such groups together. Generally, in such groups, the members read to each other what they have written and once they have learned to trust each other, they find that the comments can be very helpful. They also advise each other on new markets they have heard about, on the best typewriters and word processors, on the least expensive places to buy typing or computer paper, on events they have heard about of interest to writers for children. In fact, they become a writing support group for each other, and each takes pride in the success of the others as it comes and encourages those who may be disheartened or discouraged. From such a group there may come valuable suggestions for periodicals where you might get publication experience and publishers to whom you might want to send your manuscript. A published author with an agent may also help you if you want an agent yourself. (See more about agents later.)

You will be very lucky if you come to know a published author who could help you. But you may also find a mentor elsewhere — a librarian, teacher, bookseller, or even an editor of some sort — someone who lives near, is interested in what you are doing, and gives you advice and help as you try to develop as a writer. This person, too, may be able to give you advice when it comes time to send in your manuscript.

All of the above seems to require finding other writers, and since writing is a solitary profession, this may seem almost as difficult as finding a publisher for your manuscript. But actually it is not. The trick is to go to meetings. There are writers' conferences held in almost every state. You can find out about at least some of these by joining the Society of Children's Book Writers and Illustrators. If you have not been published, you will be joining as an associate, but you will receive the newsletter, which lists many writer's conferences (and incidently contains articles about marketing your manuscript and what editors are looking for) and you will be on the mailing list for the local chapters of SCBWI and will get notices of their activities, too. You may find meetings that you can attend where you will meet other writers of children's books. If this does not work for you, you can attend other kinds of meetings, especially those designed for children's librarians and teachers, where children's books are discussed. If these are open to the general public, other writers will be there, too. And from the sessions of SCBWI meetings or the meetings and seminars designed for teachers and librarians, you will learn what kinds of books are being written and published, information that will be helpful. Whatever you decide to do, don't stay at home writing all the time. Get out and meet other writers, talk with them, form groups with them. Don't be intimidated by others you meet: don't be overwhelmed by the success of others who have been published and try to write what and how they write. Be yourself. That's the best key to success. But learn from them and adapt what you learn to your own style and your own objectives.

There are other advantages to attending a writer's conference, over and above the writers you will meet, the group you may form, and the sessions that will give you pointers on how to make your writing more salable. Agents and editors will probably be present who will be speaking and giving advice. At many writer's conferences, it is possible, generally for an extra fee, to speak one-on-one with an agent or editor. The author is asked to submit a manuscript before the conference, and the editor or agent reviews the manuscript and gives the author advice about revising and sometimes about submitting the manuscript. Authors who ask for such an interview should be willing to hear the bad as well as the good, to think carefully about the advice given, and to at least ponder why the reader had the response that he or she did. A novice writer can come away from a writer's conference with renewed inspiration and determination to succeed, and also with some helpful hints as to how to achieve that goal, both in writing and in marketing.

STEP TWO – DECIDING WHERE TO SEND YOUR TEXT

If you know someone who has written and been published, or who knows the publishing business, and that person is willing to give you advice, follow that advice. If you have been to a writer's conference and an editor or an agent has encouraged you to send your manuscript to him or her, by all means do so. But if none of this applies to you, here are some of the things you might do.

First: If you don't have your own copies, try to borrow copies of the *SCBWI Bulletin* for the past several years and read the advice given there about publishers. Then consult writer's magazines. There are several, and they often give advice about markets for manuscripts. Much of their advice is for authors of adult materials, but some of it will help you. If you do not subscribe to any of these magazines, you may be able to read some of them at your local library. In any case, once you have done this preliminary research, check with your local library. Ask to see *Literary Market Place* and again consult *Children's Writer's & Illustrator's Market*. These publications – updated each year – list most publishers and indicate which ones publish children's books and tell how many children's books they issue each year. Next, look for the books of these publishers on the library shelves and in whatever sort of cataloging system the library uses. Since the most popular books are likely to be at someone's home being read, examining the shelves is not enough. Ask to see the catalogs of children's books that publishers send out. Most libraries of any size will have some. If yours does not, you will have to seek out one that does.

Think about your story. Then examine the types of books that each publisher issues. Does the publisher publish picture books? What kinds of picture books does each do? Which publishers publish books that are most like yours? In other words, if you have written a realistic animal story, which of the publishers you have identified also publishes picture books that are realistic animal stories? These are the publishers who will most welcome your manuscript. A publisher that issues only picture books with folk and fairy tales will not want your realistic animal story. Nor will one that publishes only nonfiction picture books. But a publisher that issues a wide variety of books and a publisher that concentrates on books like yours can be a likely market. Make a list of these publishers.

What about an agent? Should you try to get an agent? Do you need an agent? The truth is that if you are an unpublished writer, it may be harder for you to find an agent than to find a publisher. Many adult publishing departments will not read unagented material, but almost all publishers of children's books do read unagented manuscripts. Agents are useful. They know where to send manuscripts; they understand how to bring a publisher to a decision; they are accustomed to dealing with contracts. But since they make their money from the manuscripts they sell, and since — like all the rest of us — they have only so many hours in a day, they prefer to work with authors who have a publication record. So, unless you know an agent, met an agent at a conference who expressed real interest in your work, or have a friend who says her agent will be willing to take you on, concentrate on publishers first. When you are published, and when you are writing several picture books a year, for which many publishers are vying, then you will find an agent very useful, and many agents will be glad to have you in their camp.

Take your list of publishers whose books indicate they might be willing to publish your book, and look again in *Literary Market Place* and *Children's Writer's & Illustrator's Market*. This time, check the number of titles each publisher issues each year. And check the date on which that publisher was founded. Newer publishers are sometimes more open to new writers than older publishers, though this is not always true. Think about the notes you have read in the SCBWI newsletter. Take time to look again at what books you can find in the library and in the bookstore from the publishers you have selected. Which books look like the kind of book you want your book to be? Is your story one that belongs with a mass market publisher? Do you see it being sold in supermarkets and in variety stores? Or do you see your book in the library, done with handsome pictures in a large expensive format? What kind of book have you written? What is the audience for your book? Think about it not only in terms of content, but in terms of how you see the finished book — the kind of art work you would choose, if you had the chance to choose. The total look of the book. The price you hope your book will carry. On the basis of all of this, check off the publishers that seem best to you. You may even want to assign them numbers, putting the most likely publishers first.

Next consult one or another of the publications you have been using for names and addresses. Find the name of the editor of children's books at each publisher you have chosen. Write down that name and the address of the publisher. Now you are ready to send your manuscript. You have made your choice of publishers.

STEP THREE — SENDING YOUR MANUSCRIPT OFF

The first step in sending your manuscript is making sure it is in the best possible physical shape for sending. Check over your last draft. Examine the punctuation and the spelling. Look at the quality of the typing. Does it need to be typed again? Your manuscript should be typed double-spaced, or even perhaps triple-spaced. You need not (and even should not) type what you think of as separate pages on separate sheets of paper. If you wish, you can leave extra space between the sections that you think of as separate pages, but the object of your presentation is to make the whole read as easily as possible. Many sheets of paper with only a little typing on each makes for more difficult reading at the publishing house, increasing the chance that the reader will not finish what you have done. Also, the more pages you have, the more it will cost you to send the manuscript out and the larger the envelope you will need. Number the pages and put your name either at the upper left or the upper right on each page, so that every page can be identified as coming from your manuscript. The first page of the manuscript or the title page, if you make one, should include your name and address. Whether you include a title page or not depends on the length of the manuscript. A title page for a two-page manuscript seems a little foolish, to say nothing of a title page for a one-page manuscript. But a manuscript of five or six pages can certainly have a separate title page. Try to make all the pages as attractive and as blemish-free as possible.

Once your manuscript is typed in the form that you think best suits it, it is time to think about a cover letter. Your cover letter is the first thing a publisher's reader will see, so it needs to be good. Unfortunately, many people, in my experience, seem to think that "good" means telling everything they have ever done. This is not true. You do not need to tell an editor your whole life history. In fact, if you do, your letter will not be read. No editor, not even a first reader, has time for that. Yet, you should send a cover letter. It has always seemed to me that a manuscript received without a cover letter indicates a manuscript that the author does not care very much about; it is as if the author were sending a child off to school without telling the school that the child was coming.

So what should your cover letter be? First, it should be in standard business letter form: your address at the top (or following your name and signature at the bottom); the date; the inside address to the publisher, with the editor's name, the name of the publisher, etc.; the salutation ("Dear" whatever the name—and do use the editor's last name—do not address this to the first name of the editor, trying to make it appear as if you know the editor when you do not—I always hated receiving letters addressed "Dear Jean" from authors I had never met and to whom I had never written, and I assume that most children's editors feel the same); the body of the letter; then finally "Sincerely yours" (or whatever), and your signature, with your name typed below the signature.

In the body of your cover letter all you need to say is that you are enclosing your manuscript, give the title, and add, if you like, a sentence or two that tells something about your material. You need not go into your background as a writer, although if you have been published before, you ought to indicate this, and tell where and when. However, a brief summary will do: "I am the author of ten books, published by Zippo Press, each of which has won the Newbery Award and has sold over one hundred thousand copies." There is no need, as some authors do, to include a compendium of every title you have ever published. In my experience no one has ever read the three- and four-page lists of published works some authors feel it necessary to include. If your material has a special background, or if it is nonfiction, indicate your qualifications for writing, but again, do not go into great detail. One sentence — or at the most two or three — telling why you think you are qualified to write this book will do. No need for those lists of every course in the subject you have ever taken or every book you have ever read — don't laugh, people do it. All the publisher wants is enough information to indicate that you have had some publishing experience, if you have, and you have the knowledge needed to write in the area in which you have written. Remember that any time a reader spends reading your cover letter may be taken away from the time spent reading your manuscript, and it is the manuscript that must sell itself to that reader, not your cover letter.

Yet, your cover letter is, in a way, your sales pitch to the publisher. In the little that you do say, try to give the impression that you are intelligent, creative, and receptive to any suggestions that might be made to you. Do not be cute. Do not pretend that the letter is from a character in your book, introducing you. It happens! Don't draw stick figures of yourself and the editor on the letter. That happens, too! Don't do any of a hundred other cutesy ploys. They do not impress anyone. Do not be coy. Do not characterize yourself as a poor, struggling author waiting for word from the marvelous editor. Ugh!

All of which does not mean that you cannot be personal in a genuine way in your cover letter. In the brief note that you include about your material, you can project something of yourself. If you have written a mood piece about the joys of watching the dawn, you might say: "My house is located on the west side of a small lake. Each morning I view the sunrise with new joy, and it seemed to me that young children might want to think of the world as waking up each morning, just as they wake up. So I have written a short, rather poetic, I hope, mood piece about life as it wakes up each morning in my area. I think that what I have done lends itself well to illustration. If you are interested in it but think it seems too limited in approach, because it is morning at my house, I could, of course, broaden the viewpoint to include dawning in other environments." This is somewhat more than might need to be said for most works, and it is about as long as such an introduction ought to be. But it gives you an idea of what kind of information will be of interest to a first reader and an editor — information about what they are to read, what your motive was in writing the piece, and what more you might be willing to do with it.

It is even all right to tantalize prospective readers with a hint of what is to follow, to make them want to read your manuscript; but be subtle. Do not tell the reader at the publisher that he or she is about to have the experience of a lifetime (some authors do this) or ask if the reader has ever considered that one picture book — and one author — may have the solution to all the world's problems and that book now rests in the reader's hands (no one goes quite that far, but almost). Publishers do not want to be told that your manuscript is without a doubt the finest manuscript they will receive all year. They want to discover that for themselves. The joy of reading manuscripts is discovering something really good; if you want to give a reader that pleasure, don't spoil it by anticipating the discovery. Besides, if you strongly proclaim the magnificence of your work, no one will believe you. In my experience, only amateurs judge their work in cover letters.

There are other things you should not do:

Don't send sample illustrations by you or by a friend, unless you or the friend is a competent, well-known illustrator of children's books.

Don't even indicate on the manuscript what and where you think illustrations should be unless your text needs the description of a picture — or a very rough drawing — in order for the text to be understood.

Don't suggest that a famous illustrator is your choice for the illustrator of your book.

Don't engrave your envelope with silly comments about what is inside.

Don't burden your manuscript with folded-down corners of pages or other booby traps so that you can assure yourself that it has been read — if it is returned to you. (And if you do this, you can rest assured it will return. We readers and editors laugh about the devices of this sort that people use—but still, it does make us think that the author is not someone with whom we want to deal.)

All of the attempts and devices above indicate to me, and to most readers and editors, that this is a novice author. We do not have a built-in prejudice against novices; after all, every published author began somewhere, with some publisher, as an unpublished author. What publishing people object to is not new authors but authors who adopt an unprofessional stance.

If you want to be sure that the publisher has received your manuscript, include a postcard on which a reply can be sent. Many authors make it especially easy for a publisher to reply by writing a message on the card. This may simply say, *"Magic Moments in Virginia* (or whatever your title) by John Smith (or whatever your name) has been received by Allsorts Publishers (or whatever the publisher) on (leave a space for a date—it is always nice to know how long it takes the post office to deliver your work, and this information may prove helpful if you do not hear from the publisher for many months)." Below this, you can add "Signed" with another line for whoever is sending back your card to leave her or his name. This will give you the name of a person to whom you can write to if you need to check on your manuscript later. (Warning: some editors do not like to be trapped in this way, so decide for yourself if you want to do it or not.) If you don't care whether or not you know if the manuscript has been received, skip the postcard.

Your final step in the preparation for mailing your manuscript is preparing envelopes: one addressed to the publisher you have chosen and the second a stamped self-addressed envelope for return. The return envelope should be large enough to hold your manuscript. (Many times I have received a #10 envelope in which to return a 50-page manuscript—when the manuscript itself arrived in a large manila envelope.) Write your address on the return envelope clearly and put on enough postage to bring the manuscript home safely to you.

Today, when so many people are writing their books on computers and word processors, some writers do not want their manuscripts back. If this is the case with you, you will surely want to know the decision about the manuscript, even if you don't want the manuscript itself. So indicate in your cover letter that the manuscript can be destroyed, if the decision is not to publish, and include a #10 envelope addressed to you with first-class postage on it for the publisher's rejection slip or rejection letter, or possibly the publisher's letter of encouragement with suggestions for revision.

If you *do* want the manuscript back, you may need to take the manuscript, in its carefully addressed envelope, with cover letter enclosed, to the post office, have it weighed, and then put a similar amount of postage on the return envelope. Reweigh your outgoing envelope, since the return envelope may increase its weight. Seal your envelope with the manuscript, cover letter, postcard (if you choose to send one) and return envelope and put it all in the mail. Your manuscript is off and away.

Should you send your manuscript to more than one publisher at once? Should that carefully composed cover letter and perfect manuscript find its way to several readers at once? This is a question that is hotly debated in many circles. Publishers often take a long time to reply. No publisher is overloaded with readers and editors, and the number of manuscripts that arrive in children's book departments each day would be daunting even to authors who believe in quick replies. Consequently, manuscripts, even very short ones, can wait for weeks to be read. In most houses, manuscripts are registered as having arrived and then are read in the order of date received. How long it takes the staff to get to any one manuscript depends on how far behind they are in reading. This is why it takes so long. Publishers really can't help it. On the other hand, if every publisher who gets a manuscript takes a minimum of three or four months (and often longer) to make a decision, it may take a writer a long time to sell even a very salable manuscript. Authors cannot be blamed for wanting to submit their work to more than one place at once. Whether to make a multiple submission or not is a decision each author must make. It is not fair not to tell a publisher that a manuscript has been submitted elsewhere. An editor may spend a great deal of precious time — time that might be spent reading manuscripts — thinking about a manuscript and doing whatever is needed to accept the manuscript for publication, only to find that the manuscript has already been accepted elsewhere. That time spent could well have been used to read manuscripts that are still available. On the other hand, it is also true that an editor seeing that a manuscript has been submitted elsewhere may not pay as much attention to that manuscript as to another, thinking that maybe the work has already been sold. The number of multiple submissions is increasing, especially with picture books. Decide for yourself which route to take.

Whichever way you decide to go, you will probably wait. You will get your postcard back, if you sent one, but you will not get your manuscript back — or any kind of reply — probably for several months. You may hear sooner. Sometimes a publisher does get caught up with reading and can reply sooner. But don't count on it.

The best thing to do while you wait is to start on a new book. This will keep your mind off the time it takes to get a reply, and it will refresh your thinking so that if you receive a letter from a publisher that encourages your making some revisions on the manuscript, you can come to the work with a clearer mind. If you are lucky, you will get so caught up in the new book that you will almost forget the old one. Then whatever happens you can take it in your stride more easily: neither acceptance nor rejection will carry you away.

If three months have passed and you have had no word about your manuscript, it might be well to drop the publisher a note. Indicate the name of the manuscript, the date you sent it, the date received indicated on the postcard (if you sent one and if they returned it) and the signature that appears there (if there is a signature) and ask if there is any word. You can suggest that there is no reason why the manuscript cannot be held longer if it is necessary, but you just want to make sure that it has not been lost in the mail on the way back to you. (This can happen. I have known instances when authors did not inquire about their manuscript until seven or eight months after submission. The manuscript had been mailed back some months earlier, and by the time the author inquired it was too late to trace a package that had clearly gone astray.)

STEP FOUR — EVALUATING RESPONSES

When your manuscript arrives at the publisher, it will be logged in, in some fashion. Unless a publisher is not reading unsolicited manuscripts, your manuscript will eventually be read. (Materials you have read in making your list of publishers are likely to indicate publishers who are not reading unsolicited manuscripts. Then, if you want to send a manuscript to such a publisher anyway, you must write a letter asking permission to send in your manuscript. You will give a brief description of your material, send it with a stamped self-addressed envelope for a reply, and if permission comes, you can send your manuscript. Not much has been said about submission letters because for the most part publishers of children's books do not want them. It takes as long to read a letter as to read some picture book manuscripts, and writing a letter in reply takes more time than sending a rejection form.) Your manuscript will not be read first by an editor, probably. A first reader will read it — someone who knows what the editors at that publisher like and need. If the first reader likes what you wrote, then an editor will receive it for consideration. If not, you will get your manuscript back with a rejection notice of some kind.

One day a familiar-looking envelope appears in the mail. It is your manuscript come back to you. Open it. You cannot know what you will find there. Once I sent a manuscript back to an author with suggestions for revision and an indication that we wanted to publish the book. The author assumed that it was another rejection, put the envelope away unopened, and only discovered some months later that the manuscript, far from being rejected, was actually being accepted. Most of the time, as that author had discovered, a returning manuscript is being rejected. The rejection does not always mean someone at the publisher does not like the manuscript. It may simply be that the publisher cannot find a place for it on any list for several years to come. Publishers cannot publish an unlimited number of books each year. Most have a specific number that seems right, and more is too many for the staff and sales force who must handle the books. Sometimes, editors will send personal letters of regret for not accepting books that seem very good to them but that they cannot accept for one reason or another. Most of the time, however, the form letter or rejection slip is sent out.

No author should feel too discouraged when that rejection slip arrives. The best thing to do is to type a new cover letter, make out a new postcard, a new return envelope and a new mailing envelope, and send the manuscript to the next publisher on that list, made months before (unless, of course, new information has come in and another publisher now seems better than the second one on the list — or the third or the fourth if a multiple submission has been made). Send the manuscript out again, and go back to that new manuscript — or even to the second or third manuscript you have begun since you sent the first one out.

But suppose that the unexpected has occurred. You receive a letter saying that the editor likes your story, but that certain revisions need to be made before publication can be assured. Publication is not promised, but it is held out like a carrot. Follow that carrot! But do not think as you revise that you must do exactly what is asked and no more and no less. Think about the suggestions. Ask yourself why the editor wanted those changes. What about your manuscript prompted that response? If the changes would change the basic nature of your manuscript, what did you fail to do to indicate to a reader just what response you intended to get? Do the suggested changes, or the questions the editor asks, indicate holes in your material or do they indicate that you have told more than is needed? Think about it.

You are now quite removed from the work; you have, in fact, started something new that absorbs your attention, so you can look at the old manuscript with new eyes. What do you see that you want to change? How can you satisfy the editor and at the same time satisfy yourself? Don't hurry your revisions. Don't think that the editor is sitting in an office doing nothing, waiting for your material to come back. The truth is that a manuscript that comes back too fast is suspect — the editor thinks the author did not consider those revisions carefully, just did them. Editors are looking not only for good manuscripts, and people who write well, but for authors who can do thoughtful revisions.

A request for revision may make you angry at first. How can that editor think that your work is not perfect? Why should anyone suggest such ridiculous changes, or ask such absurd questions? But when your anger has cooled, and when you read your material again, you may see very well why the editor had the reaction the letter indicated. And you may even feel embarrassed that you never saw the problem yourself.

Do what you think best in revising your manuscript. Then send it back to the editor who requested the revision, indicating briefly in the cover letter that you have revised and are willing to revise further if necessary. You can again send a postcard and a return envelope, if you like, but this time it is not as essential as it was the first time. You may even get a personal letter saying that the editor is glad to have your revisions and you will be hearing further. And you will hear further. You may not even have to wait so long this time. In the meantime, keep on writing that new book — or those new books. And hope that your first sale has been made and a way has opened for the publication of your new ideas.

If you do not get an encouraging reply, however, and if you keep sending your manuscript on and get nothing but rejection slips, how many times should you send your work out? There is no good answer to this question. But after ten or twelve submissions, if there has been no indication of any kind of interest from any publisher, you should probably take another look at what you have done, and think again about the kind of publisher to whom you have been submitting your work. You might now consider putting that manuscript aside in favor of those new ones you have been busy writing.

Critique groups, writers' conferences, and simply reading magazines and other publications about children's books — even review magazines like *The Horn Book Magazine* and *Booklist* — can help you evaluate your work. Think again about the possible audience for your material. Is it too special? Is it more an adult audience than a child audience? Are your ideas too old for picture book age children? Try writing the story — if it is a story — again, using a different viewpoint, using a different level of diction. Write it several times in several different ways. Then look at the new ones and the old. How do they compare? Are the new ones better? Read all the versions to your critique group or to a trusted friend or advisor. Learn from the experience of rejection. Then put the whole thing away. Try to sell your newer works. And maybe some day you can come back to that first manuscript, and using what you have learned make of it a publishable book.

Selling your manuscript to a publisher is a matter of knowing which publisher is most likely to be interested in what you have written; sending to that publisher a manuscript in the best form possible, with a cover letter that will interest the reader who receives it, and not put that person off by overcleverness or cuteness; and by preparing yourself and preparing the way for your work. Do this by reading, by learning from others who want to write too, and by attending conferences, seminars and other events that will put you in touch with the latest ideas for selling your material and with some of the people who might buy what you have done. Most of all, however, the key to success is learning well the craft of writing.

Knowing What Happens When a Book Is Accepted

You have been writing and submitting for years. You had a strong feeling that your writing was getting better, that it was more on target, that you were finally coming to the place where maybe . . . just maybe . . . a text you had written might be accepted.

Or . . . you have written a first children's picture book text and submitted it. You have been holding your breath, trying to write something new but always wondering in the back of your mind what will happen to that first effort. You think you had a good idea, you think you did everything right, including picking the right publisher for the material — but you can't be sure.

And then it happens. You get your manuscript back and with it a letter indicating that an editor is excited about what you have done. Some revisions are requested, but it seems likely that your text is about to become a book. You can hardly believe it. After all this time . . . ! Or . . . on your very first try! Or . . . after whatever length of time it might be! What matters is that you may have sold a manuscript to a publisher.

What do you do?

STEP ONE — REVISION
First of all, you revise as requested. As suggested in the last chapter, you do not necessarily do just what has been asked and ship the manuscript back at once. Instead you think over the letter very carefully. You ask yourself why those particular revisions were requested — what was there about your manuscript that made it seem deficient in those areas? If you revise, will the manuscript come closer to the manuscript you wanted to write, or will it be a different book? If different, will you like it as well?

Will you be happy with it? If not, what can you do to keep the book the one you intended to write and still answer the revision request?

When you come to rewriting, do not just patch. Don't put the new on the old without reevaluating the old, without making sure that the whole remains a unit. Even one small change can sometimes demand other small changes to make everything fit together. For example, if Betty is going to visit Aunt Sally and stay overnight and in your original version she packed her toy wolf, but the editor suggests that a teddy bear or a doll might fit the situation and the general readership better, then Betty cannot play with her toy wolf at Aunt Sally's. And if you intended the wolf to have deep significance, somehow you didn't quite make that clear. The significance did not come through to the editor. Will it matter to you that the wolf is gone? If it does, you must find some way to make that wolf as important to the editor as it is to you. You need to use that wolf in an episode of the story so that it has meaning in the story. Betty and Aunt Sally might go to the zoo and see wolves; they might even play with baby wolves in the children's zoo. But does making that change bring the whole closer to the story you wanted to tell or does it alter the story more than the editor's suggested change? If it does, let the wolf go. If it doesn't, approach the editor with the change you would prefer, discuss it and probably your idea will win out. After all, it is your book.

Rewriting for an editor means perfecting the manuscript not only in your view, but in an editor's view as well. In regard to your Betty story, the editor may have a specific illustrator in mind, who will enjoy working with the text you have created, but who, perhaps, does not draw wolves well. Or the editor may know that in two years — or three — teddy bears will be celebrating their hundredth anniversary, and any book with a teddy bear will sell well. Or the editor may simply believe that the idea of a child carrying a wolf toy to an aunt's calls too much attention to itself, when the attention of the reader and listener should be elsewhere; it disrupts the focus of the book. The editor may explain some questions or requests, others you may have to simply deal with in hopes that what you are doing is what is wanted. Keep the book yours but do the best you can to fulfill the editor's vision of the book as well.

Work until you are satisfied. Hone and sharpen each word, each phrase, each sentence, each paragraph. But do not overdo. Don't revise until you have ironed out every bit of life the manuscript ever had. As long as you are eager to revise, go ahead; but when the whole process becomes a burden, stop. You have begun to deaden your material. At that point, make a perfect copy and send the manuscript back with a cover letter indicating that you are willing to work further if necessary. And you may be asked to do further revisions. Some manuscripts are revised three or four times before everyone is happy. One set of revisions uncovers another set of problems. Keep up your courage. And learn from what you are being asked to do. You are actually getting valuable free help with your writing. Even if in the end the editor does not take your book (which is unlikely if it goes through more than one revision), you will have had an insight into what it takes to create an acceptable manuscript.

If as you work you have some real questions about what you are doing and what the editor wants, do not hesitate to write or call the editor and ask. If there are two ways you can go with a given sequence to try to accomplish what the editor seems to want, and you are not sure which will be best, get in touch and find out. But don't worry the editor every day with new questions; don't ask questions about punctuation or other matters that are incidental to the total focus of the book. (I can recall authors doing that—and it always made me want to scuttle that author.) But if a matter affects the entire structure of the work, and you are not sure which way to go, ask.

Editors care about revision. They care about how well you revise. And they want you to take what they have said and what they have requested and use it in ways that fit what you want to do in your book. Editors are likely to reject, finally, the manuscript of an author who clearly has not thought through the revision requests but has simply done exactly what was asked and not made the revisions fit the book as a whole. Try to see the requested revisions as a chance to revisit the entire manuscript from a new viewpoint. A thoughtful reviser will make an editor happy and will find encouragement for not only one book but others to follow. When you give thought to revision, you are helping to build your career as a writer of children's picture book texts.

STEP TWO — LEARN ABOUT CONTRACTS

When both you and your editor are satisfied with your manuscript, you will be confronted with a contract. In fact, you may even receive a contract before the manuscript has reached its final stage. When you receive that contract, you will feel elated at first, and then you will feel baffled. How, you will wonder, can a publisher, whose demand seems to be for simplicity, clarity and brevity produce a document of this nature? A few publishers have relatively readable contracts, but most do not.

If you do not have an agent — and if this is your first sale, chances are you do not — then you will find that, basically, what the contract contains are the following: your promise to let them publish your book in whatever form they deem best and to handle foreign rights, subsidiary rights, movie and dramatic rights, electronic rights — any rights that might exist; their promise to give you a certain amount of money as an advance against royalties to be earned; their promise to pay you a given percentage of the cover price (or, rarely, the wholesale price) of each book sold; your promise that the work is really yours and not copied from someone else; their promise to pay you given amounts on sales of your book for all of the various kinds of subsidiary rights including foreign and paperback rights; their statements to protect themselves from you or anyone who might sue them over questions concerning the book; their statements as to what happens when the book goes out of print, or if the publisher is sold or goes bankrupt; their promise to get a legal copyright to the book in your name; their promise to send you a given number of free copies of the book when it is finally published and their statement of the price at which you can buy further copies; and a variety of other small legal points.

Because all contracts are somewhat different, and because the situations governing the drawing up of each publisher's contract can differ and make the offer contained in the contract different, it is impossible to say here just what you ought to find in your contract. Read it over, make as much sense of it as you can, and take special note of the advance to be paid, the royalties to be paid — not only on their edition but on other editions and on the various other subsidiary rights they have a right to sell. If some of the clauses bother you, consult a friend who has published a book, or even a lawyer. The problem with a lawyer is that most do not wholly understand the publishing business and raise questions that do not really matter (all at your expense). Organizations like the SCBWI and the Authors Guild can also be of help when you need it in regard to a contract. My advice is to sign that first contract, even if you have to hold your nose while you do it. By the time you are ready to sign a second contract, you may have an agent to help you, or you will have seen what the first contract did for you and what its clauses meant, and you can be ready to ask for changes on the second.

If you have really serious questions about a contract and have no one you can ask for an explanation, do by all means ask the editor to explain. Sometimes simply asking the right questions can implement changes to your benefit in a contract.

If you can avoid it, do not sign an option clause. An option clause binds you to submit your next or your next two manuscripts to that publisher (and sometimes to allow them to publish those books on the same terms as you were given in the first contract). Some authors like option clauses, which give them a feeling of security, of being wanted. But if your first book does well, if it is well reviewed, that publisher will want more manuscripts from you, option clause or not. On the other hand, if you have an option clause, the book does well, but you are not happy with the book the publisher produced, you are caught in a trap. You must send them your next book. It may be that on a first book you will not be able to escape an option clause. If you can't, you can't. But get out from under as soon as you can, even if you like the publisher and what the publisher does for you. Publishers get sold, publishers change, and you do not want to be caught when this happens.

STEP THREE – WHAT ABOUT ILLUSTRATIONS?

Do not expect to have great input into the illustrations for your book. If you expect this, unless you are a famous writer of picture book texts, or simply a very famous person, you will be disappointed. The editor and art director are going to decide who will illustrate your book. If you are lucky, they will send you samples of other work done by this artist, so you can get some idea of what may result. If you are very lucky, they may even send you samples of the art work of two or three different artists and ask which you like best. But they will make the decisions.

Not only will they make the decision about who will do the

illustrations, they and the artist will decide what and where those illustrations will be. If your book demands a special kind of accuracy — if it is a book of nonfiction or a story with a very special background or a surprise book that needs pictures to make the text work — you may be asked to supply pictures or descriptions from which the artist can work. And you may be asked to review the artist's sketches or even the finishes for accuracy. But don't expect more than that. If you do get more, be glad. If you don't, just hang on and hope for the best.

Don't let this distress you. There are several reasons why this must be so. First, the publisher has a budget for your book and must find an illustrator whose work will come within that budget. This may preclude that great illustrator you had hoped would work on your story. The budget may also mean that your book will not be the outsize 12-inch by 15-inch marvel you envisioned, but a much more conservative 8-inch by 10-inch size. And the publisher must find an artist who will want to do it in that size.

Beyond budget, however, is the whole matter of artistic freedom. You were free to write what you chose, in the way that you chose; though you may have revised to do what the editor wanted, you didn't have to do that. You could have tried to sell your book elsewhere. Now it is the artist's turn. Though it is your work he or she may be illustrating, the artist, as well as you, will be judged by the results, and will want to display himself or herself to best advantage.

As to meeting with the illustrator, publishers have found that when authors and illustrators meet, one can dominate the other. If you have very definite ideas of how the pictures should be done, and the artist knows this and tries to match your vision, the result may be a disaster — stiff, stilted pictures that please no one. On the other hand, you could be dominated by the illustrator and could be talked into changing your text to give him or her more leeway in creating the pictures — and this, too, could be a disaster. There are a few very experienced authors who work well with illustrators, who are even helpful to illustrators, but unless your publisher is sure you are that kind of author, no one will be willing to take a chance on making you a part of the illustrating of the book.

Most experienced authors know this and are used to it. They don't expect to have much to do with the pictures. I did not see the art for the picture book I wrote until it was finished and proofs had been received from the printer. A longer book that I wrote recently, which has, in spite of its length, color pictures on every page, was the same. I knew who the artist was, but I did not see any of his work until it was all completed.

When you have written your manuscript, when it has been accepted, you have done your work. Relax and go on to the next book. Let the publisher worry about pictures and budgets and trim sizes and all the disasters that can occur between finished text and finished book.

STEP FOUR – READING THE COPYEDITED MANUSCRIPT AND THE GALLEYS

Once the manuscript has settled into a finished form and probably after an illustrator has been selected, the manuscript will be read by a copyeditor. This person will check facts, spellings, punctuation and grammar and bring what you have done into line with that publisher's standard practices as far as disputed spellings and punctuation are concerned. Some copyeditors do a limited job, others do more than is requested — sometimes helping and sometimes hindering the author's intentions for the work. The author generally sees the copyedited manuscript and can quarrel with what the copyeditor has done, if this seems necessary. The copyeditor may also have attached some small slips with questions for the author. The author should answer the questions, but if there are suggestions for changes, the author can make those changes or not, whatever seems best. Most copyediting changes are minor and are helpful, but if an author believes that something the copyeditor has done harms the work, then the author has a perfect right to ask that the copyediting change not be accepted. It is best to write to the editor and point out the problem. Generally the editor will agree. In fact, the editor has probably seen the manuscript before the author and may have indicated that some copyediting suggestions are not to be accepted, even before the author has had a chance to object. Copyeditors are essential to the process of publishing, but they are not editors, and their word does not have to be final. Yet, authors should remember that the copyeditor represents a fresh, trained eye on the manuscript, and his or her reactions may be worth considering even when they seem out of line.

Once the copyediting changes have been made, the manuscript goes to the typesetter. In the case of a picture book, where type may have to be fitted around pictures, type may not be set until after the art work is completed, or at least until a firm dummy (a layout indicating the position of art and text) has been created. In other cases, the artist will want the type set before creating a dummy in order to know just how much space is available for pictures. In either case, the author gets a set of galleys to approve and correct.

It is often surprising to see how different a work looks in type from the way it looked in manuscript. Sometimes it seems like a different creation altogether. This can be especially true if, to benefit the pictures to come, the type is set in varied line lengths. However it is set, though, the author reads the galleys, finds as many printer's errors as possible, checks for other kinds of mistakes that may have been made, and then, if it seems absolutely essential, suggests other *author changes* in the galleys. These should be kept to a minimum. Your contract probably says that if you request changes in the galleys for which the cost is more than 10 or 15 percent of the initial setting cost, you must pay for those changes. And you can be surprised at how quickly those changes mount up. These days, when most typesetting is done by computer, the cost is not as great as it was when metal type was being set. Nevertheless, it is not negligible. Remember that a small word change at the start of a paragraph may mean resetting that entire paragraph. And if that paragraph has been carefully fitted to a given space on a page, a whole page can be thrown off. Read your galleys, make the changes you believe are absolutely necessary in order for your book to be as good as you want it to be, but do not rewrite your book in galleys. Your editor will be unhappy; your illustrator will be unhappy; and you will be unhappy, too, when the bill comes.

STEP FIVE—HELP PROMOTE THE BOOK AS REQUESTED

Most publishers have a department for publicity and promotion on children's books. After some consultation with the editor, the marketing department decides where your book will be advertised (not many places if you are a new author, unless a well-known illustrator is doing the art for your book) and how it will be promoted. Basically, what is done will follow a pattern of what is done for all books of the type that you have written. If it is a book primarily designed for school and library use, review copies will be sent to review media read by school and library purchasers and to some large school and library systems that still do their own reviewing. Ads will be placed—often for the entire season's list—in the periodicals such people are likely to read. If yours is a book designed for the mass market, the bookstores and whole-salers who control that market will receive copies and will be visited by the publisher's sales representatives (who will also mention any school- and library-oriented books the publisher might be issuing that season). You will have little control over what is done nationally, but you can help locally.

You will be asked for a list of bookstores where you are known or that are popular in your community; you will be asked to list newspapers and other publications that might mention your book and to whom review copies might be sent. By all means send in such information; do not overdo—your best friends do not qualify as legitimate receivers of review copies unless they review children's books for the local newspaper—but be as complete as possible. You may also be asked if you would be willing to speak to groups of adults or children. Say yes if the thought does not totally paralyze you. Getting yourself known, speaking locally, and then being asked to speak in wider and wider areas is one way that you can get out word about your book—or books.

Your job is to make people you know, people around you, even people you know in other areas, aware of the fact that you have written a book and that it is now available. *But do not deliberately go into a great many bookstores and ask for the book, even order the book, when there is no intention of buying, or ask your friends to do so.* This technique, sometimes followed by novice authors, always backfires. The ordered books will probably be returned, and the bookstore will not order your books next time, even if the requests are genuine.

If you are wise, you will not expect your first book to make enough money for you to feel financially secure for the rest of your life. This is unlikely to happen. In fact, sales may prove to be modest. What you must hope for is that sales will be great enough that the publisher will want another book from you.

STEP SIX — EVALUATING REVIEWS OF YOUR BOOK

One of the things that will help sell your book is reviews, in your local paper, in other periodicals you suggested to the publisher, and also in newspapers in large cities and in national review media. Many of these will be in publications you are unlikely to see, but the publisher will send the reviews to you. If you are like most authors, some of the reviews will make you feel very good, and some will make you angry (they simply didn't read the book — or they made no effort at all to understand what I was doing). The best thing to do is to take all reviews with the proverbial grain of salt — the good as well as the bad. Reviewers, like authors and editors and illustrators, are human beings with their own point of view, their own prejudices. What they say, whether good or bad, is as much a reflection of what they are as what you are. Read reviews, learn from them, peer beneath the surface of a review and sense what it is that the reviewer wants from a book. Reflect on both praise and criticism to see what it is that you could do to communicate better with those who read your books. Compare and contrast the attitudes of various reviewers, and then go on being yourself, but a wiser self, one who has looked at criticism, taken what applies and what helps, and ignored the rest.

You must remember, however, that reviews are the main way that many books are sold. No amount of advertising and promotion can counter a flood of poor reviews. If the reviews have been poor, do not expect good sales and do not blame the publisher for the book's poor performance. Instead, approach your editor, ask what seems to be wrong, and hope the publisher will give you another chance.

STEP SEVEN — ACCEPT WHAT COMES

No one — not the editor, not the illustrator, not the marketing people — knows what the fate of a book will be when it is published. Publishers publish books that editors and others like. They publish books that they think will sell. Why some books attract widespread attention and others, equally good, die rapidly, cannot always be appraised, but certainly the following can sometimes be responsible: the economic climate, current news reports, sudden new trends in education, and simply word of mouth, when one influential individual picks up a book, likes it and talks about it. Publishers try to anticipate and to stimulate as much favorable attention as possible for the books they publish, but more often than not the public chooses what it wants on some unforeseen basis.

Acquainting people with your book can help create acceptance for the book. But nothing you do, or others do, will in the end make the whole difference. What happens happens, and you must learn to accept this — at least on a first book and until you become better known. Sales for well-known authors can be more accurately predicted and will be more widespread, simply because people have read their earlier books and want to see what is new.

So enjoy the whole process of having a book published, do the best you can in the writing of it, in the revising of it, and in the promoting of it. But do not rest all of your hopes for fame and fortune on one book. Take publication of any book in stride, accept it for what it is, and move on.

Moving Ahead

Having a manuscript accepted, even having in hand a finished book, is no reason to rest and decide you have arrived. One book does not make a writer. A real writer goes on writing, and with ability and luck goes on publishing. So put your published (or accepted) book behind you and move ahead.

STEP ONE — DEAL WITH THOSE UNSOLD MANUSCRIPTS

If you are like most writers, that first manuscript you sold probably was not the first book you ever wrote. Many published authors began writing when they were children. One fine author told me she has a whole trunk full of things she wrote as a child and as a teenager, material no one will ever see. You may have a lot of that, too, works that taught you how to write, that developed your skills, but that now seem amateurish, works that clearly belong to your past. But what about more recent manuscripts? Do they have a chance now that you are a published writer?

Sit down and read what you have. How does it strike you from your eminence as a published writer? Are the other texts as good as the work that was accepted? If so, how many times did you send each one out? Is there a possibility that your editor has not seen this material? If so, choose the one you think is best, the one that best fits the publisher that took your manuscript, and consider it. What did you learn from working with that editor about writing in general and about that editor's tastes? Does this text need revision on the basis of what you now know? If so, do the revisions that seem right to you. Then send the manuscript to the editor, with the usual stamped self-addressed envelope.

Because you are now a published writer, your manuscript will probably go directly to the editor, not to a first reader. And it is possible that you may receive a direct reply from him or her. The manuscript may not be accepted, but it will get special attention. That is, it will get special attention if you don't flood the editor with manuscripts. Be choosy about what you send. This will keep the door open for you to that editor.

There may be other manuscripts in your back file that do not seem right for your editor, but that, nevertheless, seem to you to hold promise. Read them through, also. Revise on the basis of what you have learned in the process of becoming published. Then do as you did before: try to figure out which publishers might be interested in what you have done, study those publishers and their publications, learn the name of the editor of the department, and send in your manuscript. This time in your cover letter you can indicate that you have just published a book with whatever publisher it was. But be careful! Did you sign an option clause in your contract? If you did, you will have to submit this manuscript first to the publisher who has done your book, even when you believe that that publisher would not be interested in this particular work.

In reading through your earlier manuscripts, you will surely find some that one time seemed marvelous but now seem less than great. Put these manuscripts into your dead manuscript box and forget them, unless any contain ideas that seem worth pursuing. The manuscript can be put away forever, but the ideas should go into your idea file and maybe someday they can be used in a publishable book.

STEP TWO — LEARN TO DEAL WITH SUCCESS AND FAILURE

Not all of the reviews you receive for your first book or your ninth book or your twenty-fifth book will be favorable. Publication does not mean that the world is waiting for your book and that patrons will be breaking down the doors of bookstores and libraries to get what you have written. Yet these days it is important that a book sell well. Although it is not as true of picture book texts as it is of books for older children, it is nevertheless a fact that publishers will take one book, and then another book, and maybe a third book from a given author, but if these books do not sell, they will look long and hard at why they did not sell before taking a fourth book. The bottom line is important to publishers. They want books that sell. And so do authors. Yet, it is really the publisher's job to sell your book. And if the publisher does not, then, even though the idea that your publisher does not want another book from you may depress you, and though you may regret moving to another publisher, you may be better off for doing so.

Learn all you can about the book business. Go to the library and read *Publishers Weekly* to see what is going on. Follow other publications that deal specifically with children's books. And submit your manuscripts accordingly. Do not write to the market — that is try to write a book like one that seems to be very popular. But absorb the current trends, think about what future trends may be, based on what you know of the world and of human nature, and write works that you can write well and that seem to fit what you believe publishers will want.

Know who you are, what you want to do, and where you think you want to go. Success may come and go, but you have to live with yourself for a long time, a lifetime, and you will feel best about yourself if you put success and failure both behind you and move ahead, knowing that yesterday's triumph or disaster does not predict what tomorrow's efforts will bring. Enjoy success when it comes, learn from failure when it happens, and move on.

STEP THREE — WHAT IF YOU AND AN ILLUSTRATOR BECOME A TEAM?

Sometimes when an author and an illustrator work well together and produce a successful book, the publisher of the book will want more books by that team. No problem with that if you have other ideas that that illustrator will like. Then you will both benefit from the association. You may even find that the illustrator is someone you can come to know and work with directly — that when you both help with the creation of the idea and the finished book, a better book results. Great! Go to it.

But it may be that what worked for one book will not work for future books because it is only in one area that you and the illustrator share an interest. Unless you and the illustrator want to mine that one small interest for all that can be found there, it is better that you not become a pair. You may soon find yourself typed — as an author of books about animals of the plains or quirky modern folktales — when you would rather write books about a lot of different subjects. Don't run away from the possibility of teaming up with your illustrator again, but keep writing and submitting other kinds of books. In other words, hold on to the bird in the hand, but wing your way into the trees and the wild blue yonder, too.

If you do get into a sort of partnership with an illustrator, do not let yourself be overwhelmed by the illustrator's desire to have as much room as possible for illustration and to shape the text to the illustration. Work with the illustrator, but remember you are at least half of the team, and you have a right to write what seems most necessary to be said in regard to the subject at hand. If you and the illustrator run into real problems, remember that the editor is there to arbitrate and to try to discover for both of you what will make the most salable and the most intelligent book.

STEP FOUR — MOVE INTO OTHER AREAS

Many authors of children's books find that adults who don't understand how exciting it can be to write a children's book, how challenging such a book can be, and how successful it can make an author, often ask: "Now that you've learned how to write and have published a children's book, when are you going to write a real book — an adult book?"

The answer to such a question may well be "never." You may prefer to write children's books, and know that that is where you belong. But just because you have written a picture book story about a princess who needs to escape from a dragon, does not mean that you cannot write a nonfiction picture book about dinosaurs or a mood book about conquering one's fears of dogs or of the dangers of travel to the moon. It also does not mean that you cannot write a chapter book, a young adult novel, a nonfiction book about life on a desert island. Write what your interests and your growing knowledge of the children's book field lead you to write.

Thinking about writing several kinds of books can be especially important if you write a great many manuscripts. If you are writing six picture book texts a year, all publishable, and your publisher issues only twenty-five titles a year, it would not be fair to other writers if six of the twenty-five were yours. Besides, if your name is on six picture books all published in the same year, unless each has an illustrator whose name is famous, bookstores and even libraries are going to say, "Well, we'll take this one, but not that one." This means that all are likely to sell less well than they otherwise would. And you know what happens to authors whose books do not sell well! What can you do? There are several ways in which you can branch out.

One: you can have some of your books published under a pen name—so it won't seem as if you are writing and publishing as much as you are. You may write one kind of picture book—lovely stories of adventures on farms and in the woods—under one name, and another kind of book—retold tall tales gathered from an old relative who told them at every family reunion you can remember—under a different name—and so on. Or you can decide to write something besides picture books. You might try your hand at short chapter books designed for early readers or you might try a nonfiction book for third graders on how to behave at a family reunion, how to evaluate one's relatives.

There are many reasons for writing in a variety of formats and genres. The important thing to remember is that there is no reason why you must continue to repeat your first success. In fact, quite the opposite is true. If you keep writing the same book, you will soon write yourself out of an audience. You can continue to write picture books, or you can branch into other kinds of books for children, but you need to keep being as creative as you were when you first came into the field.

STEP FIVE—SEEKING OTHER PUBLISHERS— WHEN AND WHY

You already know that if your books do not sell, your publisher will not want to publish more of them. If this should happen to you, do not despair. Look for another publisher. Or you may be sailing ahead with your first publisher, but want to try the waters in a field of little interest to that publisher. Again, you need another publisher. Find one in much the same way as you looked for the first one. However, this time, you are a published writer. This time, you can get an agent to help you if you like. Consult friends who have agents, meet agents at writers' conferences, examine *Literary Market Place* for agents who handle children's books, and write to the one that seems best to you. If the first has a house full of authors and does not want another, try someone else. But you do not need to have an agent. After all, you did not have one when you submitted the books that were published. You can go ahead on your own. You know how to do it. It just takes time and effort, but with what you have already done and already learned, it may not be as hard this time.

Now, whether you are writing to an agent or a publisher, in your cover letter you can say that you have successfully published (all publishing is successful in cover letters) four books (or however many) with Keyhole Publishers, that you are continuing to write for them (if you are), but that you also have a great interest in writing books for a somewhat older age or for children interested in the out-of-doors or whatever the case may be — an area that does not interest Keyhole — and consequently you are seeking a publisher that will be interested in the book submitted. If you are going to do this, you can even tell your Keyhole editor what you are doing, so that if a publisher is interested in your new work, wants to make sure that you do not have an option clause that will cause trouble, and calls your editor at Keyhole, no one will be surprised.

Sometimes, too, an author-editor relationship that seemed great at the start falls apart. For some reason, you no longer seem to work well with the editor. I can recall several instances when an author seemed to be moving in a direction that was not comfortable to me — the authors found editors who were comfortable with their new directions, and I saw them go with real relief. Or perhaps you think the publisher is not doing the best job possible to sell your book. Then, you may want to look for another publisher. Editors and publishers like to keep authors and to keep publishing successful authors, but generally they are willing to let unhappy authors move on to someone else.

If you become a very successful author, it is also possible that other editors and publishers will come to you with offers, some of them so good you won't want to pass them by. But before you make such a move, consider carefully what you are leaving behind. You are moving away from a body of work to which you will not be adding new books that the publisher can use to help remind people of backlist titles, and those titles may die more quickly than they otherwise would. And think of the editor you are leaving behind. What kind of editor will you have at the new house? Will you find the kind of help you found with your first publisher? What illustrators are you likely to have in the new house? Will they be as good as the ones you have had in the past? Don't say no to good offers from others, but don't say yes too quickly either.

STEP SIX—MAINTAIN AND ENLARGE YOUR REPUTATION

No matter how many books you have published, unless your books sell extremely well, you can never be sure that a publisher will take your next book. As you have seen, if your books do not sell, no matter how good they may be, your publisher may not want another one.

Part of how well your book sells depends on how well the publisher promotes and advertises it. But the real source of sales is the book itself. If people read it and like it, there will be a core of people who know and like what you have done. If your next book is not as good as the last one, they will feel let down. The last thing you want to do is let your audience down. You want them to look for your books, to be glad when a new one appears. This will happen only if you continue to work at your writing, to improve your style and technique, and to present new and interesting material. Even after fifty books, you cannot rest on your laurels and try to relax. Not every book you write will be of equal interest or even of equal quality; no one can be perfect all the time. But each book you write should indicate in some way that you are aware of the world around you, that you are striving to mirror that world in new and true ways, and that you are improving your skills as a writer.

Authors who grow with the times and who continually improve their writing are more likely to continue to be successful than authors who discover a rut in which they can exist and who never move beyond it.

STEP SEVEN—ACCEPT THE TRUTH ABOUT MONEY

How much money will you make? That is a lively question among authors. Most write because they want to write, but they also want to make money doing it. Sometimes they do. Sometimes they don't.

You will make money if your books sell well, but the chances of your being able to support yourself from your writing—especially on those split-royalty picture books—is limited. Some authors have other jobs; some have husbands or wives who earn most of the family income. Yet, there are authors who not only support themselves but whole families on their writing; most of these have been writing for some years and their income comes not only from current books but from royalties on backlist titles as well. You may manage to do this, but even if it happens, it will not happen all at once. As a writer of children's books you are more likely to be successful, however, than the average writer of adult novels. The income of these authors is likely to be less than yours. Children's books tend to stay in print longer than all but the most prestigious of adult books, and many children's books sell better than all but the adult best sellers. This is changing a bit as the market changes and the bookstore becomes more important, but it is still true.

If you want to write, you want to write. And there is no reason why you should not hope to make money by doing so. But remember, you are choosing to be a writer. Go into it with your eyes open as far as monetary rewards are concerned. It is not the publisher's job to assure you of an adequate income, nor can you insist that anyone — or everyone — buy your books in order that you can live. You are responsible for your life, your writing, and, if you are successful, for maintaining your reputation and the continued excellence of your books. You are running a one-person business, like any other business, and if you cannot live with its uncertainties, you must either give up writing or find a way to make the money you need to live that still allows you time to write.

Being a writer is not glamorous — except in odd moments of public recognition. For the writer of children's books, there are not even fancy publication parties or opportunities to meet the great and famous. Writing is done alone and its moments of greatest joy and greatest unhappiness are often experienced alone. Yet there are rewards: the joy of seeing children enjoy what you have done; the recognition that comes from parents and teachers and librarians who tell you of the good experiences children have had with your books; the creative joy that comes simply from writing and finding a way to solve a difficult writing problem; the wonder of suddenly coming upon a new book idea that you know will work; and the feeling of accomplishment when a book is done and accepted. Money is important; no one can ever say that it is not.

Money represents readers, and readers are what you hope to have for your books. Yet there are private satisfactions that keep many writers at work, which have nothing to do with money. Try to balance these in your writing life and you will find that all the efforts of creation are worth what they cost.

STEP EIGHT — ANTICIPATING THE FUTURE

Authors who make plans too far ahead are generally left behind. No matter how successful you are with your writing, you cannot plan today what you will be writing five years from now. You will change in that time and so will the children. You may set broad outlines for yourself, but within those outlines, there must be room to move and to grow.

You must keep aware of publishing, of children, of society and its changing attitudes, but you must also keep aware of yourself. Are you nourishing the child within? Are you keeping alive your wonder of the world, your interest in what is happening, your eagerness to greet most new days? This, more than anything else, will keep you ready to write more books. Authors who regret the passing of yesterday, who deplore the fads and fancies of to-day's children, who try to hang on to the language and the ambience of the past, soon fall out of the children's book field. Children are tomorrow. They do not know the past; the world as it is may not seem perfect to them, but the perfection they seek is not the perfection of the past, not even the past of five or ten years ago.

Your job as an author of children's picture books is to remember that the books you write are the books that today's children will take into the future with them. Picture books, more than any other books, stay in the mind and help to shape the people who have encountered them. What you do must draw on the verities of the ages but must be couched in the spirit of today and tomorrow. A lot to ask for in a short picture book text? Of course. And not all texts will do this. Not every book you write must be a great book. But if you want what you write to reach into tomorrow, then you will find a way, sometimes at least, to mine the past for what it teaches, perhaps, but convert what you find into today's and tomorrow's terms, use what you find in ways that fit the lives of those who are tomorrow, the very young, and that will allow them to grasp what you do and use it for their own growth.

Children's books have a long history, one you might enjoy discovering. And we can all hope that, in one form or another, they may have a long future. Whether they do or not will depend at least partly on you and others like you, on the ability you show to keep the field viable, alive, and attractive to the very young.

INDEX

More Great Books for Writers!

Ten Steps to Publishing Children's Books—Get published in the popular genre of children's books! You'll discover vital tips from successful writers and illustrators to help you polish the skills necessary to make your dream come true. Plus, the input of editors offers a unique perspective from the publishing side of the industry. *#10534/$24.95/128 pages/150 illus.*

1997 Children's Writer's & Illustrator's Market—This directory brings together the two key aspects of children's publishing—writing and illustrating. In one handy volume you'll find helpful articles on how to make it in this lucrative field, followed by 850 detailed listings of book publishers, magazines, audiovisual, audiotape and scriptwriting markets. *#10494/$22.99/378 pages*

Children's Writer's Word Book—Even the most original children's story won't get published if its language usage or sentence structure doesn't speak to young readers. You'll avoid these pitfalls with this fast-reference guide full of word lists, reading levels for synonyms and much more. *#10316/$19.99/352 pages*

Writing and Illustrating Children's Books for Publication: Two Perspectives—Discover how to create a good, publishable manuscript in only eight weeks! You'll cover the writing process in its entirety—from generating ideas and getting started, to submitting a manuscript. Imaginative writing and illustrating exercises build on these lessons and provide fuel for your creative fires! *#10448/$24.95/128 pages/200 b&w illus., 16 page color insert*

How to Write and Illustrate Children's Books and Get Them Published—Find everything you need to know about breaking into the lucrative children's market. You'll discover how to write a sure-fire seller, how to create fresh and captivating illustrations, how to get your manuscript into the right buyer's hands and more! *#30082/$24.99/144 pages*

The Very Best of Children's Book Illustration—Feast your eyes on this wonderful collection of the best in contemporary children's book illustration. You'll see nearly 200 full-color illustrations sure to spark your creativity. *#30513/$29.95/144 pages/198 color illus.*

Writing for Children and Teenagers, 3rd Edition—Now in its third edition, this comprehensive guide gives you the up-to-date information you need to get published in the ever-expanding field of children's writing. *#10101/$14.99/272 pages/paperback*

Grammatically Correct: The Writer's Guide to Punctuation, Spelling, Style, Usage and Grammar—Write prose that's clear, concise and graceful! This comprehensive desk reference covers the nuts-and-bolts basics of punctuation, spelling and grammar, as well as essential tips and techniques for developing a smooth, inviting writing style. *#10529/$19.99/352 pages*

The Writer's Essential Desk Reference—Get quick, complete, accurate answers to your important writing questions with this companion volume to *Writer's Market*. You'll cover all aspects of the business side of writing—from information on the World Wide Web and other research sites, to opportunities with writers workshops and the basics on taxes and health insurance. *#10485/$24.99/384 pages*

The Writer's Digest Dictionary of Concise Writing—Make your work leaner, crisper and clearer! Under the guidance of professional editor Robert Hartwell Fiske, you'll learn how to rid your work of common say-nothing phrases while making it tighter and easier to read and understand. *#10482/$19.99/352 pages*

How to Write Attention-Grabbing Query & Cover Letters—Use the secrets John Wood reveals to write queries perfectly tailored, too good to turn down! In this guidebook, you will discover why boldness beats blandness in queries every time, ten basics you must have in your article queries, ten query blunders that can destroy publication chances and much more. *#10462/$17.99/208 pages*

The Writer's Digest Sourcebook for Building Believable Characters—Create unforgettable characters as you "attend" a roundtable where six novelists reveal their approaches to characterization. You'll probe your characters' backgrounds, beliefs and desires with a fill-in-the-blanks questionnaire. And a thesaurus of characteristics will help you develop the many other features no character should be without. *#10463/$17.99/288 pages*

The Writer's Digest Character Naming Sourcebook—Finally, you'll discover how to choose the perfect name to reflect your character's personality, ethnicity and place in history. Here you'll find 20,000 first and last names (and their meanings) from around the world! *#10390/$18.99/352 pages*

Writer's Encyclopedia, 3rd Edition—Rediscover this popular writer's reference—now with information about electronic resources, plus more than 100 new entries. You'll find facts, figures, definitions and examples designed to answer questions about every discipline connected with writing and to help you convey a professional image. *#10464/$22.99/560 pages/62 b&w illus.*

Creating Characters: How to Build Story People—Grab the empathy of your reader with characters so real—they'll jump off the page. You'll discover how to make characters come alive with vibrant emotion, quirky personality traits, inspiring heroism and other uniquely human qualities. *#10417/$14.99/192 pages/paperback*

The Writer's Digest Guide to Manuscript Formats—No matter how good your ideas, an unprofessional format will land your manuscript on the slush pile! You need this easy-to-follow guide on manuscript preparation and presentation—for everything from books and articles, to poems and plays. *#10025/$19.99/200 pages*

Beginning Writer's Answer Book—This book answers 900 of the most often asked questions about every stage of the writing process. You'll find business advice, tax tips, plus new information about online networks, databases and more. *#10394/$17.99/336 pages*

Make Your Words Work—Loaded with samples and laced with exercises, this guide will help you clean up your prose, refine your style, strengthen your descriptive powers, bring music to your words and much more! *#10399/$14.99/304 pages/paperback*

Voice & Style—Discover how to create character and story voices! You'll learn to write with a spellbinding narrative voice, create original character voices, write dialogue that conveys personality and make the story's voices harmonize into a solid style. *#10452/$15.99/176 pages*

Getting the Words Right: How to Rewrite, Edit & Revise—Reduction, rearrangement, rewording and rechecking—the 4 Rs of powerful writing. This book provides concrete instruction with dozens of exercises and pages of samples to help you improve your writing through effective revision. *#10172/$14.99/218 pages/paperback*

Freeing Your Creativity: A Writer's Guide—Discover how to escape the traps that stifle your creativity. You'll tackle techniques for banishing fears and nourishing ideas so you can get your juices flowing again. *#10430/$14.99/176 pages/paperback*